DECOLONIZING TRANS/GENDER 101

DECOLONIZING TRANS/GENDER 101

B. BINAOHAN

biyuti publishing
Toronto

Dedication

this is for my chum.
ur a fucking unicorn.
and i love you a lot, ok?

message to the generous souls who supported biyuti publishing

as promised by one of the perks for biyuti publishing's May 2014 fundraiser, this is a special dedication/acknowledgement to four people who put their faith into a small press and, by extension, all of its writers (including me!)

thank you so very much.

you very much truly and sincerely have made this book possible by supporting my work.

so...

thank you to:

Mitch Kellaway / Rasiqra Revulva / Jessica Saenz Tenneyuque / Carly Kocurek

Contents

Acknowledgements

i'm not even sure how to thank all the people who've contributed to the ideas in this.

i'll do a quick list or something.

but first, i'd like to thank nica and FrankE for beta reading the manuscript and adding their comments. you've made this book so much richer and awesome by gracing it with your words/ideas.

a lot of the people who've influence my ideas in this book are on tumblr. whatever. here is a list of people:

- sofriel
- blackfoxx
- strugglingtobeheard
- riley
- christine
- anagrammaton
- rubato
- tala
- girljanitor
- ipit
- titotibok
- angrybrownbaby
- rumplestiltsqueer
- imnotevilimjustwrittenthatway

er... this is who i can remember off the top of my head. but this list shouldn't be understood as complete.

thank you all for continuously challenging me to think harder and be creative.

1. Introduction

1.1 Motivation

The motivation for this book partially arises out of a request I received from a fellow Filipin@ who wanted to know if there were any good Trans 101s devoted to Indigenous and/or People of Colour's (IaoPoC) genders. I couldn't think of a single one off the top of my head. I ended up writing a fairly quick (relatively) blog post about it. And, for the most part, I was content to leave it at that.

Until I saw a recent publication, Transgender 101: A Simple Guide to a Complex Issue (2012) recently published by Columbia University Press and written by Nicholas M. Teich.

The book purports to be an accessible introduction to 'transgenderism' and the issues surrounding the identity. Except...

And this is where it gets especially problematic, one of the things it claims to do is touch upon the 'history' of transgender. Except, it is impossible to talk about the history of transgender with no explicit mention of colonialism or race. [1]

How can we talk about transgender without locating the identity in a larger global context? Or without mentioning the way that these guides, intended and whose purpose is explicitly to simplify complex issues, erase experiences of many people, while normalizing others?

Where is the transgender 101 for all the people who are erased, omitted, marginalized, left out, by guides like this? It is clear that there needs to be something more. Something for the rest of us. Something that allows us to have a conceptual space where we can articulate our experiences. And articulate them in ways that do not make us feel false or incorrect for all the ways we do not see ourselves reflected in the white normative trans/gender discourse.

---

1. Fe -- why does 'history of transgender' sound so odd to me? I know it's the use of the term, which, thinking of our convos and stuff I've seen from you, this isn't your wording but this Teich guy's. It feels like 'transgender' as strange entity, and not an adjective to describe the experience(s) of of actual people.

I, of course, have a personal and vested interest in something like this. And in the process of decolonization.

My very first blog post was about the colonial nature of white trans/gender discourse. It was at a time of personal awakening for me and a time when I was beginning to separate myself from all kinds of white rhetoric and discourse.

I ended up encountering, early on, this bit of history of the San Francisco Trans March

> We are calling for this march to demonstrate that we are a significant and growing portion of the lgbtiq community; to increase our visibility and presence in the tgiqlb community and the overall community at large; to encourage more trans and gender-variant people to come out; to build connections among ftm, mtf, bayot, crossdressers, sadhin, hijra, transvestites, bantut, drag queens, drag kings, mahu, transsexuals, bakla, travesti, genderqueers, kathoey, two spirit, intersex and those with other labels for themselves and no labels for themselves...
> 2

It had never really occurred to me, until I saw this, that the trans community was under the impression that it was including people like me. Or that I was, as far as they were concerned, part of their community.[3]

Imagine my surprise (no really, try to imagine it). And it wasn't as if, up to this point, that I'd never encountered or spoken to white trans people before. I had. I had friends, dates, etc. in the community (since I was never really one to exist within the white normative/assimilationist part of the cis queer community).

Except... up to this point, I had been IDing largely as gay. And this remained true, even in my younger years when I had a very femme presentation (skirts, makeup, etc.). This situation was plausible because, in my community at least, this is what 'gay' meant.

2. San Francisco TransMarch. Accessed April 4, 2013. http://www.transmarch.org/about
3. Fe -- I wonder how many folks of color for whom the white discourse makes no sense experienced this? Since this is also apart of my narrative.

Of course, the Tagalog word for it is bakla (or sometimes is, at least). It was only after realizing that I'd never been gay, but rather bakla, that I saw the SF Trans March's pseudo inclusion of my identity under their umbrella. Their laundry list of Indigenous and/or people of colour (IaoPoC) genders as an attempt to appear inclusive.

(and i now know there is a certain amount of irony, at least, of including bakla in that list for an event like the Trans March)

Yet. This is exactly the problem:

What is behind the failure of the trans community to actually be relevant to someone like me? Someone they appear to think should be under their umbrella? [4]

And, of course, part of the problem is books like Teich's Transgender 101.

The problem lays in all of these white attempts to explain, educate, and reduce the complexity of a complex subject for those who oppress us.

(I do understand the motivation, btw, I just don't buy into it. Because these attempts are usually predicated on the notion that it is necessary for us to be understood by our oppressors if we ever want them to stop. Except… what is actually necessary is that oppressors remove the hate from their hearts and see those they step on as human beings. Understanding isn't necessary.)

This reduction and simplification, ultimately ends up normalizing one way to conceptualize gender. One way for it to be articulated. One narrative. One story. [5]

It invokes the danger of the single story, as explained by Chimamanda Adichie in her July 2009 TED Talk[6]. And it is dangerous indeed, particularly, for IaoPoC people struggling with our gender. [7]

---

4. not always by name, but it is pretty clear that I'm often considered to be a member of a community that rarely, if ever, leaves actual space for either my body or my voice

5. Fe -- and of course that one way is the white way.

6. http://www.ted.com/talks/chimamanda_adichie_the_danger_of_a_single_story.html

If you look at the recent report, Injustice at Every Turn: A Report of the National Transgender Discrimination Survey [8], it is apparent that IaoPoC trans or gender non-conforming people face levels of oppression that far exceeds that of white people. It is even more stark when you look at the list of trans deaths posted by the Trans Day of Remembrance every year and see that, by and large, most of the horrific transmisogynist violence is directed towards trans feminine IaoPoC. [9]

Books and blog posts, etc, like Teich's 'simplify' these struggles away. They create a mythical reality where all of our experiences are the same and equivalent. Even worse, they attempt to present them in a pretend method that is allegedly 'accessible.'

But they never ask the important question: to whom is this book supposed be accessible? Because, beyond the obvious answer that the guide or Trans 101s generally are intended for a cis audience, they should also be useful to people at the beginning of their journeys.

To all the people who type into Google "am i trans?" and hope to get some sort of answer to the this pressing and important question. Because this stuff is the foundations for communities. It defines the discourse and impacts not only the conceptual space available but also the allocation of very needed resources. [10]

---

7. nica -- this is, in some way, unrelated to this part of the text, but maybe mention in footnote that Adichie's work has also recently been critiqued for transmisogyny, citing essentialist biological notions of sex/gender-conflated

8. (#footnote-33-4 "Injustice at Every Turn: A Report of the National Transgender Discrimination Survey. 2011. http://www.thetaskforce.org/reports_and_research/ntds"

9. Fe -- I swear I used these exact sources, and this exact connection in my senior capstone paper. now, seeing this I realize how much I was still trying to prove my humanity and that of everyone who was kind enough to allow me to share their experiences with my professors and the internal review board.

10. Fe -- I never searched 'am I trans.' I didn't think that term, even when identifying with another white term genderqueer, included me, It was so, medical. I ended up dropping the white term I was using because it was so "I'm rebelling against my parents' world."

b. -- omg. yes. i definitely, ought to have mentioned this too. i never googled this myself either. and this book really is for all of us who might have never (and maybe still haven't) thought about ourselves in those terms.

The community and available resources are critical for ensuring that more of us lead successful lives in ways healthy and happy. To allowing many of us to survive. And for us to go beyond survival.

To reach a place where we can be free. Of oppression, of violence, of racism, of cissexism, of transmisogyny, of transphobia, of colonialism.

Just.

Free.[11]

---

11. nica asked me to clarify what i mean by this. to a large extent that prior paragraph stating freedom from oppresion... but not freedom from our identities about those integral parts of who we are and that shape our embodied experiences in the world. Like. I want a world free of transmisogyny but not of trans women of colour. i fervently do not believe that 'trans woman' depends on cis ppl (or transmisogyny or oppression) to be a coherent category of identity. in a world without transmisogyny, there will still be trans woc and cis woc. all that will change is that twoc die or be punished simply for existing. but we will still exist.

1.2 What to expect/how this is written

Now, because, the inaccessibility of white trans/gender discourse remains one of its biggest problems. I mean... this is why we need trans 101s and why there really is a need to have something that, non-academics can actually read and understand[1]. Or, if not in academic type speak, something that is findable (since there are many accessibly written things out there, but they can be rather scattered and disparate. leaving people to sort of... weave together a tapestry. which does, have its benefits, since people can create the picture/story they need but then again... sometimes this stuff can be hard to find. particularly if you are IaoPoC and all can see how our voices get drowned out in the cacophonous noise that is white discourse).

Anyway. Accessible. This isn't meant to be an academic book. i imagine, that some ppl out there will end up using it for that purpose. fine. But i'm definitely not writing with that audience in mind. sometimes, depending on what i'm talking about... my tone might be more jargony and academic. often, i hope it'll be a lot more casual than that.

as a result, i'm not planning on engaging a great deal of academic texts or articles. I might cite them occasionally, but they won't be the focus of the discussion. and hopefully, when I do engage them, i'll do a decent job of explaining what they are about and what is happening.

of course, i do understand that some people will still find either my writing or manner of speaking inaccessible. restrictions of language (ie., writing in english but not another language). the fact that, as much as i may like to, there isn't a great deal that i can do about the fact that I've 11 or so years of being in university/academic contexts. undeniably, this will creep into my writing and some will not be able to access the ideas. my apologies for that. it is likely the case that some people may not enjoy the casual tone or the fact that this book will likely have gone through conceptual editing but that most errors

---

[1]. and this is not about assuming anything about the intelligence of trans people, but rather knowing that something like this should be readable by a trans girl who dropped out of high school because high school

of grammar and/or spelling won't be fixed (and, occasionally might be on purpose) because i don't really care to follow the conventions of english anymore. Or. I will do so tactically and with purpose (which also means... that if i catch people citing this book and correcting grammar or sticking in [sic] i'll be massively unimpressed.)

RE: citations and shit. i imaging that there will be many times that i present an element of the discussion as fact or without much to back it up. This generally will mean that I'm expressing a truth about the world as i see it. it may be a conclusion i've drawn from stuff i've read. from piecing together histories and facts. it may be something that i learned long ago but can't remember where. Without a doubt, there'll be many places of error and simply factually incorrect statements. fine. I don't actually care about this because, in many ways, this will be about my personal journey of decolonization (a process far from complete at this point). [2]

Nonetheless, since this is supposed to be, to a certain extent, an explication of basic notions and ideas for decolonizing trans/gender theory, i'll do my best to explain and make clear my reasons for asserting whatever belief or opinion I might have about something, especially if I understand that not everyone may follow.

But this is different than when i might refer to a historical fact without reference. For example, Chinese people invented both paper and the printing press. gutenberg or whatever didn't actually do much that was special, other than introducing this technology to white people. the first book ever printed in China was the Diamond Sutra. These are things I've learned in my readings and life. This is both history and fact. Anyone person with the internet can look it up and confirm whether or not i've spoken the truth about the printing press. One thing this book isn't, is a history book. these sorts of things will underlay the discussion and some of the things I say.

2. nica -- adding this comment after having just finished the book: at first i wasn't sure what you meant about personal journey of decolonization. but it became clear in the conclusion section. though i'm sure someone could read this and wonder what you mean, or even question if you are reducing decolonization to a personal act or using it in a general way at this point in the text -- this could also just be me reading into this, since certain parts of the 'decolonization is not a metaphor' article are in my head and it's generally received a lot of attention- meaning it might be something some ppl have in mind while reading yr text[footnote]

some of the readers of this book, may actually learn more not from the book itself, but through their personal investigations of the claims that I make. This is, without a doubt, one of the best ways to learn. Moreover, since this represents my thoughts and knowledge up-to-date i fully expect that even just one year after publishing i'll have changed my mind about some of the content. or learned more. or, the best case scenario, one of the super awesome people reading this book will contact me and help me on my journey by correcting some falsehood or whatever.[footnote]Indeed, i've already been working on this book long enough that my opinions and thoughts have changed on some of the earlier contents, which i may annotate in footnotes

Most especially, re: That last point, nothing i say within should be understood as a definitive, stable truth. anything and everything is open to revision. I have zero desire to set myself up as some authority on trans/gender theory from a decolonization perspective (this is actually, yet another reason that I'm not pursuing traditional publishing avenues. since if i were to get this published by, for example, a university press this would give the book a veneer of authority that would be false, beyond simply contributing to the white academic industrial complex).

I'm not an expert. I'm a person trying to understand themselves.

Lastly. One of my previous educational areas of interest was logic. I know a great deal of logic. and about argumentation. It wouldn't be a false statement to consider myself a philosopher. Who knows? This book could potentially be considered a work of philosophy. Anyway. The point I'm making here is that I usually know if I'm making a sound and valid argument. You may not find a lot of that in this book. I may even contradict myself.

White logic and white rhetoric is one of the very first ways that we allow our discourse to be colonized. Because, as any real logician knows, there is a plurality out there of logic. There are many logics and this stands out against the more popular and normative understanding of logic (and, by extension) rationality. If anyone attempts to engage this book or its writer (me!) with a notion of talking about how illogical, irrational, or poorly argued it is, they'll have failed in one of the most central aspects of what this books hopes to achieve: decolonization.

for some (maybe many) this book will present itself as incoherent, stilted, broken, uneven in style.

there are probably more than a few errors (although... if there is a place or sentence where it appears that i've said something really out of character or contradictory, it is most likely because i've forgotten a negative somewhere -- this tends to be a common grammatical mistake that i do.)

the book is imperfect: as am i.

1.3 About me

As with any personal type work as this one, it is and will be useful for everyone who reads this book to have an understanding of who I am and what the context of my articulation of these ideas is.

It is a little weird for me to be writing this stuff when i've done so much at this point to... protect my privacy and stuff. Mostly because life, being what it is, means that at this particular stage, I'm really rather vulnerable and can't really afford to be as visible as I'd like.

Anyway. It is, however, important for me to sufficiently describe enough of my history so that people understand my context so that they can situate the ideas and stories in this book within that context.

I was born in calgary alberta canada. for those who know canada they'll recognize alberta as being, what is not so affectionate, 'little texas.' This is mainly to highlight the sort of commonalities in terms of oil culture, rednecks, and cowboys (i mean, the calgary stampede is still a big thing, essentially calgary's big claim to fame and the biggest tourism event that the city has).

What is related but, perhaps swept under the rug, when this stuff is being discussed is how calgary (and alberta as a whole) is also a ridiculously conservative place. it is, with no contest, the most conservative place in canada. all the provincial governments have been conservative since i was born. they, especially outside of the urban centres and often within them, vote consistently conservative at the federal level too.

It is the place where the premier, after the supreme court had already rendered its decision, said that same-sex marriage would never be allowed in the province (only to capitulate at the last minute because... well, he actually knows how the canadian judicial system works and knows that after the supreme court decides something is unconstitutional, there was little choice in the matter).

Related to this overall conservatism is, of course, all the conservative values of white supremacy, cissexism, sexism, ableism, fat phobia, etc etc etc.

This is where i grew up.

I also grew up in a single parent home raised by my Filipino dad. My mom is white (french canadian). They both speak english as a second language, which is the main reason why i only knew english growing up. because even though my parents divorced quite early, my dad never got into the habit of speaking Tagalog at home.

To, in a very quick anecdote, explain or sum up the sort of family life i had growing up:

It is part of our family lore that the reason why my dad, man of colour that he is, managed to get custody over my white mother — in the 80s no less — is because he threatened to kidnap my sister and i. he would take us to Manila where he'd raise us and my mom would never see him again.

The alternative, but not conflicting story, was that he used my mom's lack of education against her by tricking her into signing away her custody without her knowing what she was doing. Given that she was essentially fleeing an abusive relationship,

It is hard not to believe that a combination of the above actually did occur.

Obviously my dad was awesome growing up.

On top of growing up in a Filipin@ household, it is also the case that i had more contact with my Filipin@ familiy in calgary than i did my white family. I've still, to this day, only seen my white family a handful of times. This is largely the reason why I only ID myself as Filipin@[1].

(the other part that is important about having my particular Tagalog dad is that it very much was me growing up in a diaspora. my dad

1. er... well, Tagalog to be precise since I share the belief that legitimizing my colonizer's name for me isn't really the way to go

is fiercely nationalistic. gave me a copy of nole me tangiere by Jose Rizal, that i never read because he — for no apparent reason — never actually told me who Jose Rizal was and why this particular book is so important. i've now given away this book b/c i didn't know what it was and wish i had it back because I actually really want to read it now)

The reason why this is important — my being mestisa — and growing up in very racist calgary is that in calgary i very much had light skin privilege but was definitely a visible minority. with people making fun of my chinky eyes (or straight out using that slur). continuous questions of the 'what are you?' kind. People constantly asking if i was either Chinese or Japanese.

This shaped my understanding of myself in relation to the rest of the world. And my understanding of how I see myself.

Which is also why it was a surprise that after i moved out of calgary to a city with more diversity, and more Asians in particular, that I suddenly started to meet people who were surprised that i am Tagalog.

It took me a while to actually mark this transition. where I went from being visible to invisible. To the shift from light skin privilege to white passing privilege. and, of course, hindsight being what it is, i can definitely better see the difference that this transition made in my life.

So racially, that is sort of where i'm at.

in terms of gender. the situation is a little more complex (and perhaps) interesting.

But i guess more of this story will unfold itself as i go along in the book, since i'll primarily be using my own experiences as examples for how trans/gender 101 needs to be decolonized for all the ways that it was essentially impossible for me to see myself in the type of narrative and structure prevalent in Teich's book.

But here is how i currently ID.

I'm a Tagalog bakla. These are my preferred words to describe myself.

When I need to use white/anglo words for myself these are the ones i'm reclaiming and are okay with

ladyboy, third gender, transpinay

in terms of the first two, especially ladyboy, unless you're SEAsian, i do not want anyone using that word to describe me. the word is rooted in racism and transmisogyny and while i've chosen to reclaim the word for myself, it remains a slur coming out of the mouths of white people. okay? third gender, while not a slur, is similarly racist and while i'd be okay-ish with other people using it… the preferred one for other people is either:

bakla or transpinay

okay?

anyway. this is me.

you might be wondering what i'm doing writing this book if i don't even ID as 'trans' to begin with.

the main reason is: is that while i may not see myself as having space or representation in the trans community, i've definitely come to learn that the community has been (falsely) thinking it has been including me. this is a serious problem. and this book. more than anything else, is an exploration for understanding how this disparity in perception is possible.

1.4 Language

1.4.1 on 'trans feminine'

for the most part, i mostly talk about trans women. but often trans feminine people too, as a way of being somewhat more inclusive to girls like me [1]

eta: this isn't really true for me these days. but. whatever. i am both at the same time. transinay as third gender ladyboy and transpinay as woman.

i had a discussion with a trans woman about the desirability of using trans feminine, rather than trans woman. her concern (and it is a fair one) was about the colloquial conflation of 'feminine' with 'femme'. whereby 'trans feminine' can evoke a certain... almost mandatory and very specific notion of femininity.

and, yes, this most certainly is a concern.

part of the distinction, here, is just grammatical. 'woman' is a noun and 'feminine' is an adjective. 'feminine' in its vanilla (re: dictionary) meaning simply means 'of or relating to women'. [2]

the logical conclusion of this should be:

anything a woman does is feminine. anything at all. [3]

however, in a cissexist world that enforces essentialist notions of womanhood, the converse is usually assumed to be true

any person embodying femininity in some way, is a woman [4] [5]

---

1. my particular ID as a transpinay ladyboy =/= woman. not for me, anyhow.

2. totally reading vanilla as white, since that's what the dictionary definition is anyway

3. The exception here, of course, are those woman who choose to embody masculinity in whatever way they want

4. the obvious exception here: since we are discussing essentialist notions of womanhood: one cannot properly said to 'embody femininity' unless that person is white, able bodied, neurotypical, thin, middle - or higher - class, born with a certain body, etc. etc.

5. Fe -- and there it goes, lol

english has many limitations. and here we bump into one of them.

because when we look at the global scope of #girlslikeus we need some way of speaking generally without imposing identities on other people. this is particularly the case since queer people decided to make such a strong distinction between sexuality and gender, and this distinction is oft upheld by trans feminine people.

when we look globally, we can locate a bunch of people and identities who, when reading reports/studies/research, are often labelled as 'trans women'. but, of course, this is an ill-fitting and, more importantly, imperialist translation of a great variety of genders.

the risk of doing otherwise is continuing to create a space where someone like me, will never feel completely at ease in. it took me so long to find the community because i never realized that it was here for me. and i'm not alone, in this regards.[6]

and it is an interesting and dangerous place to wander into. since i am impacted by transmisogyny. my life has been governed and controlled by it.

so too are the many trans feminine people worldwide. many of whom are bearing the brunt of transmisogynist violence (most of the murders of trans women of colour do not take place in europe, canada, or the usa).

i like 'trans feminine' because it is an adjective. We have trans feminine people. And the space within 'person' is large enough to encompass and include more people than 'trans woman'. It allows for the people thus classed to name and identify themselves.

1.4.2 Update on 'trans feminine'
i've seen a bit of discussion recently on tumblr abour the usage of 'trans feminine' and/or 'trans femme'. It has been a few months since I wrote the previous section and figured it was time for an update since my perspective on it all has changed somewhat in the ensuing months and discussions.

6. Fe -- Yes!

At the time, I generally asked around to see how others were referring to the community as a whole... there wasn't much consensus, which is totally okay. I think at that time, I largely settled for the nominal phrase of 'the community impacted by transmisogyny' or something similar for when I need to use a shorthand method to refer to, well, the community of people impacted by transmisogyny.

I also made a critical error (actually two) in that post.

First was not making clear that the post was about how/why **i** use trans feminine, rather than making a proscriptive suggestion for how other people should refer to the community. Then (and now) I have little desire to see anyone mold themselves to my notions of language. Nor do I even necessarily think that consensus is necessary or desirable.

As an example, not too long ago a bunch of ppl jumped on me when I linked to a story that involved a South Asian organization that had 'sh****le' in the title. I neither censored it nor trigger warned for it. My reasoning then (and I still stand by it) is that if this is how the organization and members wished to refer to themselves, then it is fine by me. If this was the term they found empowering and that allowed them to achieve their goals and aims, again I have nothing to say about that. I neither think that they should change their name to something less cringeworthy in a north american context nor do i think that any NA orgs should be compelled to use that word for themselves.

Second error (and this is the major one) was framing the discussion as if 'trans feminine' should supplant 'trans woman' (or whatever) as the better/more inclusive option. Not only was this misguided, it is definitely a sign of my internalized trans misogyny. And since I've come to embrace my trans womanhoood, I definitely understand why 'binary' TWoC I know were.... not very impressed by the post.

What it should have been about, was using 'trans feminine' as a **supplement** to trans woman when it makes sense, a la "trans women and trans feminine ppl". Not 'trans feminine' _instead_ of 'trans women'. On my part, it was an act of erasure towards a community already much erased from the movements it has started.

As for when it makes sense to use 'trans feminine' rather than 'trans women' really are those cases where you read about a murdered 'man' found with women's clothing, but no name is ever given and the identity of this person is just… unavailable. This happens a lot in global news, you look at last year's TDoR list and there are a lot of missing names. And since many of these events occur in PoC places which may or may not have their own way to denote the gender of the person, this is a context where I prefer to use 'trans feminine', so as not to impose an ID on the person.

But also to make it clear that the person is part of the community of people whose lives are impacted by transmisogyny.

Which actually ties into the discussions I've seen recently on 'trans feminine' and seeing people use it who do **not** belong to the community of people impacted by transmisogyny. A cis woman who may have transitioned to being a guy for a while does not count as this.

While I generally attempt to avoid speaking of birth assignment, this is one of the times when it is necessary, since dfab violence towards the community impacted by transmisogyny is real. Moreover, trans men already have a long history of invading women's spaces. It would not be either safe or acceptable for a dfab person to show up to a space for trans women and/or trans feminine ppl. Indeed, it would just be another example of dfab violence towards us.

Trans women have so **few** spaces given the way we are systematically pushed out or excluded from most of them. Indeed, I'd hazard to say that most 'space' we are able to take up is largely conceptual. So. Yeah.

This applies with 'trans femme' as well. I was recently surprised to see someone who I thought was a trans woman and/or trans feminine person (but used 'trans femme') actually just say that they were a man. Which… what. IN part, this is largely an issue of syntax. If this person had said 'femme trans man', i likely wouldn't have made the mistake. Or even 'trans femme _man_' and I probably would have got the right message. Otherwise, I totally understand 'trans femmes' to refer to the subset of trans women and/or trans feminine ppl who ID as femme. So, likewise, if I were to go to some probably **awesome** trans femme of colour event, having a man show up would be jarring and, well, make the space feel decidedly less safe and welcoming.

I'll leave off with a reminder that this all is about my current engagement with these terms, and not prescriptive. No one else is required to use language in the exact ways that I do (I don't even think this would be a good thing). Just where I'm at right now, okay?

2. What is 'transgender'?

2.1 The word and its origins

The root of the word transgender comes from the Latin word trans, meaning 'across.' A transatlantic flight goes across the Atlantic Ocean; a transnational issue affects people all across the Country; and so on. Transgender literally means 'across gender.'[1]

Transgender is defined today as an umbrella term with many different identities existing under it. Some of these identities, such as gendervariant, genderqueer, and cross-dresser, are covered in chapter 8. We are going to put those aside for now. The type of transgenderism that we are most concerned with in the bulk of this book is transsexualism.[2]

Of course, because this is meant to be a 'simple' guide for those nice, well meaning cis people, this is all we get for what transgender means. And. Yeah. It is a very boring sort of definition that also doesn't do much for really understanding what it is supposed to mean. Not really.

He does do the kindness of giving some of the context in which 'transgender' becomes a coherent identity. Explaining things like the gender binary and such. Also giving the basic outlines of the supposed differences between sex, gender, gender expression, gender identity, etc etc. [3]

You can also see from the quoted paragraph that he is going to focus on transsexualism (glob, this fucking term hurts my brain) as a special kind of transgender sub-category of the people who identify as the opposite sex of what they were assigned at birth [4]. Now. Based

1. Page 2. Teich, Nicholas M. Transgender 101: a Simple Guide to a Complex Issue. Columbia University Press, 2012.
2. Page 2. Teich, Nicholas M. Transgender 101: a Simple Guide to a Complex Issue. Columbia University Press, 2012.
3. and, of course, he can't quite seem to pull it off without making some unnecessary reference to the Black american community on page 3
4. Teich 2012, 3

on the super confusing and conflating discussion that follows, it is unclear how we are supposed to understand transgender people who ID as the opposite gender (since, Teich explicitly notes that transsexuals do not need to have had any kind of surgery in order to be a transsexual, which is contra the what many people in the community think especially along the lines of the True Transsexuals).

But. Let us not pay attention to the man behind the curtain!

Instead, lets look at a short history of the word so that we can understand when it came about and why it was considered necessary:

> In the early 1990s, 'transgender' was repurposed by a various groups of transsexuals in the US to basically include anyone whose gender expression was non-conforming with society's expectations. There were several reasons for this and one of them was because people with atypical gender identities do not always identify as transsexual.... [5]

Between this post, and Part Two [6], we can see that 'transgender' was a consciously and purposefully chosen term to be broadly inclusive of pretty much all the white genders and a variety of expressions out there. It was intended to serve a political utility for uniting a diverse group of people to fight with solidarity out of shared interests for the same sorts of social goods

(social goods like: anti-discrimination in housing, health care, employment, etc. or for having easier access to changing documented genders/sexes. or just the right not to be murdered in the streets. you know, high faluting stuff like that)

Put in another way: transgender was intended not to supplant something like transsexual but to compliment it. Except. As with Teich's explication, it becomes rather difficult to understand what

---

5. Denise Norris 2011a. http://transgriot.blogspot.ca/2011/12/on-being-transgender.html
6. Denise Norris 2011b. http://transgriot.blogspot.ca/2011/12/on-being-transgender-part-ii.html

the exact difference between transgender and transsexual is. (anyway, more of this discussion is continued in the next section).

Understanding the history and motivation for 'transgender' as political and social umbrella is key for understanding all the ways that it left people sitting out in the rain.

It is also important to understand that, in common usage today and for how most people interact with this term, not all variance in gender expression is actually included in 'transgender.' Like. Butch lesbians? Rarely group themselves in this category. Or how about femme gay men? Or crossdressers? Or drag queens/kings? Not so much. [7]

Perhaps one of the biggest things needing to be decolonized about this explanation is the way that it overrides individual identification out of a need for a hegemonic identity for the 'common good'. [89]

(and, yeah, i realize that in decolonial terms, it is often considered white/western to emphasize the individual over the community. but i would answer this challenge with: no. I don't think that it is coherent to say that all IaoPoC people are to be understood as collectivistic in ways that replicate the situation we are currently discussing. Because the understanding, especially speaking as a Tagalog, that we are collectivistic in ways that leave little or no space for self expression is a racist and colonial notion of what it means to have a community centred on the community, rather than white individualism). [10]

7. Fe -- should there be a note here about how class and race affect what these identities mean? Like, for example, as you mentioned earlier, the word gay in some black and brown communities was an umbrella term (and where I am) that included many if not all of these, especially gay, dragqueen, crossdressers. Also these are sometimes used interchangeably or as additional adjectives to an identity? but wait, you probably address this later, and this is really still and investigation of how Teich is arguing.

8. Fe -- The white good. I am going to end up saying white a million times.

9. b. -- ah, but i love be exact and precise and it matters a lot for this sort of thing to be super specific

10. Fe -- Stating that collectivism and individuality can exist within a single community is so, so very important, and I also feel addresses that either or colonialist thinking, when we are far more diverse and complicated than that. We can be both/and or something completely different and a lot of this is situational, adaptive, human? shutting up now.

one of the few axioms of the current (mostly) white trans community that i actually agree with is that self identification comes first.

So. If we take this premise, we should understand that transgender people are those people who ID as transgender. And the transgender community is the community of people who ID as transgender. If this seems rather circular, it isn't. Since this is actually the way that classes or sets are classically derived from predicates. If person X is transgender, they belong to the set or class denoted by 'is transgender'. But a person can only be transgender if and only if they identify that way.

This is actually and absolutely necessary to preserve the autonomy and agency of people. As such, it actually runs contrary to the definition as it was also described by Teich.

Since the other problem with both definitions is that they depend on legitimizing one type of experience over others, since the definitions rest on a common or shared experience of (more or less) not IDing with your assigned birth gender. Or whatever. Except, by doing so, they create an identity and community that roots itself on exclusion and policing, since you then become 'transgender' insofar as your own experiences are able to match up with this standard, normalized narrative.

In many ways, the basic point to be derived or understood in this section is about what it means to be transgender. And what it means is that at some point, you sat down and said 'I'm transgender' and nothing else. Many people might be surprised or resistant to the notion that being transgender actually has nothing at all to do with gender. or sex.

but, honestly? it doesn't. especially not if we are understanding it as some umbrella term.

Because at the end of the day: if you are a man, you are a man. If you are a woman, you are a woman. if you are bakla, then you are bakla. if you are agender, then you are agender. These are the actual genders. But having any of these genders do not defacto slot you into the umbrella group of transgender.

It is a standard tactic of white rhetoric to generalize (and thereby reduce, erase) identities and categories. This is standard. This is how I went from being Tagalog to 'Asian.' What is even more standard in white rhetoric is insisting that this kind of erasure by generalization is necessary in order to achieve an real solidarity for working towards freedom. [11]

Is it? I don't really have any great answers for this question, especially i do know that having or using these labels can be quite freeing for many people. And, this is a good thing. Moreover, it is definitely true that many of us do not (for whatever reason) have direct access to our cultural heritage. And. so.

What else are we left with but to use words like this? (and, again... even if you find utility out of MtF, this doesn't not necessarily mean that you have to consider yourself 'transgender').

I guess i could try and actually give a decolonized 'definition' of what 'transgender' is:

Transgender: A hegemonic socio-political identity crafted by (mostly) , white[12] binary trans people. [13]

Its purpose? To erase the individual and unique struggles of various communities so that people like Teich can claim the oppression of groups like TWoC to bolster his/their claims of being super oppressed and, thus, being able to centre their voices in discussions about gender equality. [14]

---

11. Fe -- i.e. in order to make it so all of the voices and the organizing and the issues solely address white struggles and maintain a system of white supremacy and colonialism.

12. added this to partially address Fe's comment, since i don't think that iaopoc were much involved with this

13. Fe -- were trans indigenous and/or people of color involved in this process? This makes it seem like a yes, and clearly people not yet decolonizing, or who were able to identify with what I perceive to be a very specific class, race, and regional narrative?

14. Fe - gasp is an inefficient word to describe my elated shock knowing that this is stated so openly, and so boldly in a text that will be accessible to my friends and family.

2.2 Current Irrelevant Debates

2.2.1 Transsexual vs. Transgender

In the previous section I mentioned the strangeness of Teich insisting that he was focused on transsexualism as a special subset of transgender. But. Of course, the distinction between the two was rather confusing and it doesn't follow the usual understanding that transsexuals are binary ppl who've had both HRT and SRS. This is, at the very least, the distinction that the True Transsexuals would have us believe.

And it is the source of some of the context for the posts I linked to on transgender as an umbrella term, since the True Transsexuals usually take the stance that they are not transgender. for some reason or other that i've never been able to figure out.

Mostly because I really don't care. This is rightly the first entry for 'irrelevant debates'. The people sitting on either side of this debate (be they white or IaoPoC too enmeshed in this colonial discourse to see outside of it) tend to forget that each sides is equally supporting a colonial discourse that outright intends to be transmisogynist.

The choice of sides are:

- transgender: people who are (from the quoted post above) perfectly willing to enforce a hegemonic identity that values 'political unity' over self autonomy and agency.
- transsexuals: people who believe that only binary medicalized genders are valid

Looking at this... is it any wonder that this debate most often seems to occur between white people? or that it is unsurprising that Teich finds invoking this rather unnecessary distinction for his book unproblematic as a white trans man?

Especially for the ways that each side of this debate, in addition to the debate itself does absolutely nothing for trans feminine IaoPoC?

It doesn't help any of us gain better access to resources for expressing and embodying our genders.

It doesn't help any of us gain better access to resources we need to live (ie., jobs, housing, social services, etc.).

I can't even bring myself to adequately explicate what this debate is about. Mainly because I've never understood. Moreover, I don't care. Everything I've heard about this makes me care even less.

Because no matter who is ultimately 'right' or who 'wins' the losers, at the end of the day, remain

us.

2.2.2 Sexual orientation vs. Gender

Since this irrelevant debate is worth of an entire chapter in Teich's book, we'll be discussing it at a little greater length than the transsexual vs. transgender debate. However, more time spent with this discussion does not actually make it less irrelevant.

Teich writes:

> Sexual orientation relates to someone's romantic and sexual attraction to another person. [1]

Okay. Sure. We've already covered what transgender means. So I guess we can see how these things aren't quite the same things. The real problem comes with this statement:

> But, as we know, understanding transgenderism as distinct from sexual orientation is important. [2]

but. like most of this book. he never really posits or answers the question: to whom is this understanding essential?

because if we simply take my own gender as an example, bakla, we can see that this ID as is commonly used encompasses both what would be considered 'gender' and 'sexuality' in white western discourse. except because it doesn't reside within white gender

---

1. Page 14. Teich, Nicholas M. Transgender 101: a Simple Guide to a Complex Issue. Columbia University Press, 2012.
2. Page 15. Teich, Nicholas M. Transgender 101: a Simple Guide to a Complex Issue. Columbia University Press, 2012.

discourse, it actually represents a continuum of different genders, sexualities, and gender expressions all of which are covered by this one word.

in many ways, this is also what gay used to mean, if you go back far enough. more importantly in some IaoPoC communities gay is still used in this way today (see Imagining Transgender by David Valentine if you need a white academic source that discusses this).[3]

But. It is important that it is a white trans man who is asserting that this distinction is essential.

Because it is, as we can see from the history of the gay and lesbian rights movement, a distinction that was necessarily enforced by cis white gays and lesbians with the sole purpose of ensuring that the trans feminine IaoPoC people who started the movement were systematically pushed out, excluded, and erased.

This distinction continues to serve white men like Teich because it helps them solidify a hegemonic discourse, like the book he produced, that makes it hard or nearly impossible for IaoPoC to articulate their genders. [4]

This serves to ensure that the trans/gender movement follows the same path as the gay and lesbian movement: essentially enforcing a discourse designed to co-opt and erase the voices of trans feminine IaoPoC.

So. Yes. This distinction is important for a man like him and for all the other white produced trans 101s out there because saying anything else would open the doors of the movement to actual diversity and maybe, just maybe do the very necessary job of decentering of white voices in the movement.

and, really, nothing better demonstrates the irrelevance of this discussion than Teich's own treatment of it.

3. Fe -- Yup, yup. yup. I thought this might come later.
4. Fe -- I admittedly did not read Teich's book, but the idea that he finds a need to draw that line, to push that agenda of cis masculine skinny upper middle class gay white boy kind of screams, "see I'm just like you" in the same way gay inc screams to their cis straight cousins.

He actually, for real, I'm not even joking here. Brings up the antiquated kinsey scale of all fucking things [5]. You seriously can't even make shit like this up. Anyway, for those who don't know, the kinsey scale represents another instance of that white mania to quantify everything, in this case sexuality. It is old and bullshit. This is all you really need to know.

And I could discuss the rest of the chapter, but is even more irrelevant, rehashing the old arguments amongst lesbians and trans men that does nothing, really but cement just how transmisogynist both communities are.

2.2.3 dysphoria as defining quality of being trans

i started this book maybe over a year ago (today is may 13, 2014) and in just in the past few months i've been seeing a *lot* of discussion (usually trans women vs. trans men) about the fact that

'you aren't really trans if you don't experience dysphoria'

which, of course, is utter shit and completely wrong. many of the people (and, no, it isn't just trans men) pushing this as the defining experience of being ~trans~ are relying on the recent replacement of 'gender identity disorder' in the dsm iv with 'gender dysphoria' in the dsm v.

now. insofar as one is attempting to obtain trans related healthcare in an area following the wpath standards[6], yes, you should make it clear to your healthcare provider that you experience 'dysphoria'. lie if you have to. then again, nothing about lying to your health care provider re: your actual gender is anything new to people who've been navigating the medical industrial complex.

but what of the claim "ur not trans if you don't have dysphoria"

in most of the discussions i've seen dysphoria is *strictly* understood as body dysphoria only (not social dysphoria, spiritual dysphoria ONLY body dysphoria). which. lol, whatever.

---

5. Page 18-22. Teich, Nicholas M. Transgender 101: a Simple Guide to a Complex Issue. Columbia University Press, 2012

6. these are discussed in greater detail in a later chapter

first major problem with this view is that it entrenches a white supremacist worldview. the basic definition of 'body dysphoria' basically asserts that a person's internal sense of gender is at odds with (in some non-trivial respect) to their physical/outer body. that is, this relies on a form of mind/body dualism quite common in white philosophy but most certainly *not* universal.

however, if you are operating within a worldview that asserts that the mind and body are a single whole, we suddenly loose this frame of reference. we cannot talk about an 'inner' conception of gender vs. an 'outer' physical body. it is incoherent, since there is not 'inner' and no 'outer', simply one complete, unified mind/body.[7]

there is no coherent way to articulate body dysphoria within a worldview that has no distinction between mind and body.[8]

and, sure, one could assert that this simply means that individuals embodied in such a worldview, regardless of whatever they do or feel, can never be 'trans'. and while there is something desirable about this stance, since it would mean a critical disruption of white trans imperialism in discourse, it is also a case of shutting the gates after all the sheep have fled.

given that white hegemony over trans/gender discourse is pretty much the *point* of this book, such a stance isn't useful. especially since the advocates of this position are *wrong*.

particularly if we look at it from an historical perspective: many of the historical examples in iaopoc gender systems we have of people anachronistically often called 'trans' are people who pre-date the current trans/gender discourse.

---

7. strangely, it suddenly occurs to me that even in the white worldview there is a tension here, since to a certain extent it is this exact 'break' between mind/body that could be the underlying motivation for treating transness as being 'disordered' or as a mental illness, despite the fact that one can only follow this path if you are already using a framework in which the mind/body is something that can be separated

8. although, i should really note that if the worldview has a holistic mind/body but also room for spiritual/religious stuff, it can allow for a tension or discord between inner spirit vs. outer body, HOWEVER, most indigenous gender systems i have any familiarity with don't usually treat any 'difference' between spirit and body as ~discord~ or something that is ~wrong~ and needs to be fixed.

it also entirely removes considerations of power in this. and what purpose it serves for certain white trans people to insist upon this conception of trans.

Moving on.

3. Coming out

3.1 The closet as myth

To a certain extent, this book is intended to be a general criticism of Teich's book. But there is no way to engage his section on 'coming out' without reifying the fiction of the closet as a universal 'trans' experience. Not only does he take it as some de facto thing that trans people necessarily do, but his handling of the topic is largely trite and uninteresting (barely touching on the differentials of privilege and danger inherent with entering the topography of the closet for IaoPoC).

Instead, I'm going to talk quickly about how the 'closet' is a social construction and what this construction is. And how it fits into the larger context of white hegemonic discourse.

The closet is a social construction relative to the white society that created it (largely white/anglo north americans). Being based not only in whiteness but in the 'developed' 'western' world as is the case, this means that as a construct it is neither universal nor separable from the historical context in which it was constructed.

Rather. We can see that the construction of the closet relies heavily on the public/private distinction so crucial to whiteness (and capitalism as it happens). There is a great deal of feminist criticism on the public/private dichotomy that I won't reference here because (obviously) too tainted with transmisogyny to be of much use. What is really important to know is how the public/private distinction is one of the many results of colonialism and the development of capitalism.

Why? Because a notion of 'private' is absolutely necessary for there to be private property. And land, property, is the foundation of settler colonialism and the economic systems it has built[1]. Before the things like the french revolution, the industrial revolution, before colonialism, 'private' property essentially did not exist in europe. in the age of absolute monarchs and feudalism, all land technically belonged to the monarch (with obvious variations depending on

---

1. the other foundation for colonialism and our current economy is anti-Blackness and slavery

region and people). the monarch was the entity who granted rights for certain people (nobility) to make profits and occupy the lands. the monarch could take away this land if they chose.

It isn't for nothing that at the beginning of the colonial age, the explorers claimed lands in the names of their monarchs. because at this time, claiming personal ownership over land wasn't really something people did unless they were royalty (this is why we have the Philippines a land claimed on behalf of king philip of spain). go forward a few hundred years as the notions of capital, ensuing revolutions, continued colonialism, and suddenly the notion of private property becomes a central thing to our current society.

for racial relations, this is clearly important for the ways that only white people were allowed to have 'private' lives. they were the only ones who could own land. and, even more starkly, people. Because it is also under this system that some people are 'public' and some are 'private'. And it is clear from the way that the Atlantic slave trade happened, that Black people were considered public. This clearly links ideas of agency to whether or not people can be construed as 'private.'

This is important because the topology of the closet rests on this foundation. What is 'in' the closet is private, personal and what is 'out' of the closet is public. The process of coming out, then is a process by which you render what is personal, public. [2]

And this is an interesting place for any IaoPoC person. Because we all know, growing up and around, that our 'closets' are much much much smaller than any white person's (and it only shrinks with the more kinds of oppression you experience). Because being a non-white body in this world, is to immediately be rendered available for public consumption. where white people will feel comfortable discussing or commenting on your body. touching it (for a very notable example, see Black women and their hair). sexualising it. desexualizing it. or any other activity which clearly lets us know that we are not entitled to the same level of body integrity and 'privacy' that white people are.

2. Fe -- I don't think I have ever come across this stated in such a way. It kind of exploded that whole gay white boy claiming an inner Black woman, thing. It also makes me think of the unauthorized touching and questions I've seen witnessed regarding the genitalia of predominantly trans women, and most recently Black and brown trans women.

This level of publicness comes with a great deal of problems. particularly for dark skinned Black people and/or Latin@s (these sorts of things definitely exist on a sliding scale of dark/light skin, where the darker you are the more public your body). [3]

And it is in this context that all trans IaoPoC are given the expectation that we be 'out'. [4]

to a certain extent, we can see the problems with this construction, since it really comes down to an expectation that we render our bodies even more available to the 'public' for consumption [5].

And we are expected to do this despite the mounds of evidence that doing so will only increase the chances for Black and/or Latin@ trans feminine people of experiencing violent oppression. The same is true to a lesser extent for other IaoPoC trans people.

so. part of the message for this section is:

It is never wrong to prioritize your safety

one interesting consequence of the invocation of the private/public dichotomy in closet discourse is the ways that it ends up glorifying white individualism (or exceptionalism) over and above any other concerns.

3. nica -- to consider: i recently saw a conversation on my dash, strugglingtobeheard reblogged it, summarizing that a South Asian, specifically Indian person, with darker skin mentioned that there is a difference between 'Indian dark' and 'African' dark -- positioning the latter as worse than the first- so not only is darkness that thing by which a person is rendered public- but specifically Blackness, in congruence w the logics of chattel slavery, is of course the category from which one should distance themself. this doesn't contradict what you have written- but comments on what Lewis Gordon, has said, I think something like "above all, don't be black"

4. and, of course, i'm not even touching upon the incoherence of what the fuck it even means to be 'out' as a gender. a trans woman is a woman at all stages of her life -- unless she states otherwise

5. and, as should be clear right now, the 'public' is white people, esp. cis whites but also white trans ppl because they also participate in the consumption of public iaopoc bodies -- almost recursively seen in the necessity of this book, since if white trans ppl weren't actively perpetuating a hegemonic gender discourse and actively colonizing the bodies/ narratives/culture of iaopoc, this book wouldn't be necessary

we see movie after movie after book after narrative about trans (and/ or queer) coming out stories. and in all these narratives coming out is framed as this individual action that occurs in opposition. In opposition to (most often) family, to religion, to social communities, schools, etc. Etc.[6]

it assumes as very white notion of valuing the individual's needs above that of their communities. which, on its own, is fine. but the problem comes in when people are shamed for choosing to subsume their needs to that of their community's. Things like this come out with 'national coming out day'. or with the urging of famous (rich white) celebrities telling everyone that they owe it to the trans/queer communities to be 'out'. [7]

and that implicit responsibility is interesting looking at it from a transpinay point of view:

because my experiences in either the trans community or queer community have made it very clear that the 'community' is hostile to my existence.

and so the request to sacrifice my current communities, the communities to which i properly belong, just to fulfill some (imaginary) obligation to a community that regularly lets me know how much i don't belong, seems ludicrous. but it is not just that: it creates a situation whereby not only is the white trans/gender narrative normalized but your value/goodness as a human being becomes dependent for how well you are able to locate yourself within that narrative.

and, of course, all of this ends up being 'be out' for the good of the public. but who is this public? it is the rare person who actually bothers to mention how being 'out' for iaopoc actually benefits our communities. like, don't even get me started on how many times i've seen one iaopoc group or another mention that all this gender/ sexuality/identity stuff is white stuff.

---

6. Fe -- I hope you go on to address this linear path connected to coming out, and the kind of stagnation of ones identity, because I have yet to actually meet someone Indigenous and/ or of Color whose experience actually went a to b to c.

7. Fe -- It also assumes that the individual's needs and their identities can be above or beyond, or disconnected from the community.

which means that if we reify the closet just to come out we are, in part, validating this criticism (since we accept a white framing for our genders and histories) but also being — on a very deep level — disavowed by our communities, since this is something white ppl do and if you aren't white and doing it, you've been around too many white people and no one should have anything to do with your self-colonizing ass.

of course, we know well that there are a wide variety of iaopoc cultures that have more genders and different gender systems than white ppl. and this includes 'newer' cultures that make space for gender variance without explicitly marking it. or that many communities embody colonial imposed binary genders in very different ways than white people. all of which happens in a space beyond coherence for white discourse.

3.2 Closet as empire

but of course, the construction of the closet doesn't stop here. it's foundation may be the public/private dichotomy, but its framework is the moral implications associated with it. But the morality of the closet is a sleight of hand. it is a lie and a trick.

the clearest moral associations with the closet involve honesty and openness. if you are 'in' the closet you are dishonest. if you are 'out' of the closet you are honest. this is a large part of white transgender narratives, this feeling like they are hiding and tired of living a lie.[1]

very little room is in this narrative for people who are simply not operating within this moral space. for people who have greater considerations than personal feelings of dis/honesty. the standard white narrative about this insists that you are better off being 'honest' and losing your family, rather than staying 'in' and keeping your family.[2]

of many things, this has the consequence of erasing the experience of many IaoPoC people for whom family is a very important part of their lives (it really was for me). It also removes any chance of having a nuanced approach to who we chose to disclose what parts of ourselves to. Because there is nothing wrong with not telling your family stuff while disclosing yourself socially. It goes on. We exist and move through many spheres of life (personal, professional,

1. Fe -- I also read this closet dichotomy as being out equals healthy and liberated, being in means unhealthy and oppressed? because all you need to do to escape your oppression is to be out.

2. and, really, let's be super honest here... it requires a certain level of economic and social and racial privilege to claim that disposing of one's family is a sign of moral integrity. for good or ill, for many poor iaopoc our families are literally the only support system we might have for quite some time. we often can't rely on friends (that much) because many of them tend to be in the same position and not really able to help. getting jobs is harder. getting housing is harder. accessing social services is harder. it isn't for nothing that the loss of family for many iaopoc trans ppl results in homelessness or having to work in underground economies. white trans ppl do face this... but iaopoc (when they aren't the majority) are vastly over-represented. and for us... we don't actually have piles of media showing us the wonderful lives awaiting us outside the closet... not when most twoc appear as sex workers, dead, or monsters.

social, filial, romantic, etc.) and whatever decisions people are making about in which of those spheres disclosure is safe and desirable are 100% okay.

so I repeat:

IT IS NEVER WRONG TO PRIORITIZE YOUR SAFETY

Interestingly, if we undercut this very white notion of the closet, we also end up removing the need to engage some other contentious (but also irrelevant) debates in white trans/gender discourse.

This, chiefly, are the discussions about 'stealth' 'passing' whatever. It is fairly common to hear 'x person is stealth' or 'y person passes' and as others have noted, this type of discourse with gender doesn't really make any sense. When a trans women is perceived and treated as woman, based on the choices she has made regarding her presentation, she is not 'passing' as a wonan. Simply because she is a woman. Just as, before she started modifying or changing her presentation/body/whatever she was still a woman. Passing in this context is largely incoherent.[3]

But what of stealth? It still is incoherent because it is basically used to say that a trans women being treated as she is, but not disclosing her being 'trans', is being stealth. Except... A trans woman telling anyone that she is a woman (or people assuming such based on her presentation) isn't 'stealth'.[4]

Even more dangerously, this notion places an implicit expectation that trans people should be disclosing their histories to everyone they meet, regardless of circumstance or consideration to personal safety.

3. not to mention that it is also a framing that relies on erasing the historical specifity of 'passing' within the Black community. Wherein passing as white really was a thing, but the examples/cases/phenomenon make it quite clear that passing is a conscious choice to be something you are not. this isn't the case here.

4. Fe -- I've never encountered the term stealth. This could be due to the trans community I was involved with being much older. I also can't help but to wonder if this is a term often applied to trans women, and/or those who experience transmisogyny which I do not. It feels like that transmisogynist trans women trick cis men bullshit, and makes me wonder of it's origins.

To a certain extent, these notions exist because of a somewhat needed discussion that occurs around transmisogyny (and transphobia) about what it means when your presentation/gender and how people perceive and treat you is aligned in the expected ways (in other words, your presentation as a woman is aligned with cissexist notions of what a woman looks like and people treat you accordingly). One can almost perceive the utility of this, because it is fairly well known that the more visibly trans you are as a woman, the more direct and overt transmisogynist oppression you'll experience.

Interestingly, though, one of the consequences of framing this discussion around ideas of 'passing' or 'stealth' rather than visibility, is that it has the effect of blaming victims. Because it legitimizes a discourse wherein a person comes to expect that the better they 'pass' the less transmisogyny they'll experience. it puts the onus on trans women to conform to cissexist notions of womanhood rather than on transmisogynist people to adjust their ideas of what women are. Ultimately leading to the conclusion that visible trans women are at fault for not doing a better job at passing, should they experience oppression in some fashion.

this is also yet another imperialist and assimilationist aspect of white trans/gender discourse. Since it inevitably turns out that a person's ability to 'pass' depends on how closely they can approximate or embody white standards of beauty, since cis white women are understood to be the very pinnacle of femininity and womanhood. And, of course this is an impossible standard for any trans feminine IaoPoC to meet. Because try as we might, we'll never be white.

3.3 the closet as reified white worldview

in section 3.1 i talked about the topology of the closet the in/outs of it, so to speak...

in that section, i related it to larger social/historical contexts about the public/private spheres. however, their is also a personal, individual level of this narrative that serves to entrench a white supremacist worldview of the body and self.

namely... the spatial orientation of the closet, the distinction between what is 'inside' and what is 'outside' reinforces that white myth of mind/body dualism.[1]

this is a part of that narrative of gender within white trans/gender discourse that asserts that being 'trans' is about a disconnect between the self's inner perception of gender and the outer, public interpretation of their body. this is the 'i'm a woman in a man's body.' While this has become somewhat out of fashion... the framing hasn't and despite a shift away from this particular phrasing, this narrative is alive and kicking.

Indeed, if we look at the definition of our good friends, the HRC[2], this is how they are defining 'gender identity':

> The term "gender identity," distinct from the term "sexual orientation," refers to a person's innate, deeply felt psychological identification as male or female, which may or may not correspond to the person's body or designated sex at birth (meaning what sex was originally listed on a person's birth certificate). [3]

1. No, whites aren't the only ones with this in their philosophy but their formulation of it relies heavily on christian morality, something that feeds into the moral dimension of the closet i discussed in section 3.2

2. this is sarcasm, okay? the HRC is not a friend to trans women.
http://transgriot.blogspot.ca/2007/10/why-transgender-community-hates-hrc.html

3. http://www.hrc.org/resources/entry/sexual-orientation-and-gender-identity-terminology-and-definitions

This is a pretty standard definition. standard enough that the current 'trans rights' bill in canadian parliament, Bill C-279, has almost an identical definition:

> In this section, "gender identity" means, in respect of an individual, the individual's deeply felt internal and individual experience of gender, which may or may not correspond with the sex that the individual was assigned at birth.[4]

See?

there are many problems with this...

first. it reinforces the medicalization and pathologizing of gender.

within this mind/body split, what ends up happening is this. the disease is 'transgenderism', the symptom dysphoria caused by this disconnect between inner gender and outer body, and the 'cure' is hormones and gender confirmation surgery.

the end goal being, full reintegration of the transgendered subject into white cissupremacist society.[5]

second. it creates the 'true transsexual'

with the standard being above... we reach a point within the community that unless you fit precisely into the above, you aren't really trans. idk, you're going through a phase or something. you are a 'transtrender.'

and it is strange (but not really) that this construction ends up alienating and excluding a lot of iaopoc. why? because our narratives don't necessarily fit into this model. and this is often especially true for those of us with cultural and historical backgrounds of so-called 'gender variance'.

---

4. http://www.parl.gc.ca/HousePublications/
Publication.aspx?Language=E&Mode=1&DocId=6256603&File=24#1
   5. I go more into the pathology of being transgender in chapter 6. one but needs to look at the WPATH standards of care to know that this is the end goal -- one happily supported by HBS'ers the world over

this construction leaves no room for people and peoples with worldviews that have a more holistic approach to the mind and body.

third. the problem of individualism.

mind/body dualism also tends to put the genesis of gender wholly within the individual. it removes the social aspect of things.

and by this, i don't necessarily mean 'social dysphoria.' rather, i'm pointing to the iaopoc cultures that i know of where 'trans identities' were historically a community focused role. that gender is/was a combination of both invidual agency but also social community.

this sort of thing, of course, was/is really only possible within those cultures that have more than two genders, who had a more complex gender system than whiteness typically allows or considers coherent.

all of this runs together to privilege white narratives and white trans/gender notions about gender and how it relates to the body.

4. Transition

4.1 Socially

on the surface of it, this section of Teiche's book seems fairly straightforward and unproblematic [1]

Except... that it really does have a lot of problems with reifying cissexist notions of gender. While this is ultimately a problem he has with a large portion of the book: an insistence that 'trans' can only be articulated or intelligible in relation to 'cis'.

For example:

> during transition, many transwomen experience — for the first time in their lives — what it is like to be treated as a woman [2]

I would be surprised if there was any possible reading of this paragraph that doesn't end up with the implication that before transition a trans woman isn't actually a woman. this cannot help but be completely essentialist.

More dangerously, it taps into the 'socialization' weapon so often wielded by radfems against trans women.[3] The myth of socialization is a damaging one.

And it is a myth.

For saying that a trans women wasn't being treated as a women before transition leaves us with the implication that there is some universal or shared socialization that men have and women have. That somehow, beyond belief or reason, a trans women is socialized as a man, rather than as a woman. That a woman's experience of

---

1. Page 45. Teich, Nicholas M. 2012. Transgender 101: a Simple Guide to a Complex Issue /. Columbia University Press.

2. Page 45. Teich, Nicholas M. 2012. Transgender 101: a Simple Guide to a Complex Issue. Columbia University Press.

3. And I wish I could be surprised to see a trans man using this, since this implicitly benefits him, since it is most often used as the excuse for allowing trans men access to women's spaces while barring trans women.

being in a particular body and being forced to act in ways contrary to her nature, is invalidating because people have erroneously identified her gender her entire life.

this of course leads into his rather clueless discussion of the loss/gain of privilege that comes along with being perceived either as a man or a woman.

just so we are clear:

if you are a woman, you have never had 'male' privilege.

if you are a man, you have always had 'male' privilege.

it doesn't matter if you are trans and have transitioned. any tacit privileges you may have had or lost, were never really yours to begin with. when you break the white/cis supremacist bargain of gender, you quickly come to understand just how conditional the privileges you once had are. or how conditional the privileges you gain are.

er…

anyway. social transition is, more or less 'coming out' (see previous section for why this is shit).

and. yeah. working towards fully embodying your gender and finding a presentation that suits you and makes you happy isn't easy.

moreover, for trans feminine IaoPoC, it can be incredibly dangerous. especially if we are talking about Black and/or Latin@ people.

it isn't easy because we've already failed to be acceptable women because we aren't white. and this makes the steps we take towards embodying our genders and living authentically incredibly difficult.

but we should also take a moment to understand and think over why invoking the myth of socialization is not only damaging (as noted above) but also how it explicitly serves to exclude trans women from women's spaces and how it colonizes gender discourse with a virulent type of whiteness. [4]

it is unsurprising that a white man like Teich is sure to tell cautionary stories about reading too much into the man privilege that trans men have. and why he'd assert that

> "It doesn't seem fair to say that either transmen or transwomen have it easier' [footnote]Page 47. Teich, Nicholas M. 2012. Transgender 101: a Simple Guide to a Complex Issue. Columbia University Press."

Mainly since he has a vested interest in maintaining the socialization myth and pushing the fiction that it is 'unfair' to say whether or not men or women have it easier [5]

just so that we are very clear: trans women have it harder. trans men have it easier. and the reasons for this being the case is not much different for why women (trans or not) have it harder than men (trans or not). misogyny is a real thing in the real world. And since misogyny achieves its purest and most violent form with transmisogyny, it only stands to reason that it is not only fair but accurate to say that trans men have it easier than trans women.

if I were so inclined, I could support my claim in the previous paragraph with the vast amount of statistical data, anecdotal data, biographical data, research data, etc. etc. that gives us the fine details of what, exactly, it means that trans women have it harder. I could do this, but I won't bother. the evidence is all around. and it is most visible and explicit at every single trans day of remembrance event that takes place.

---

4. Fe -- Considering the blank slate ideology that goes along with socialization plus the notion that children are innocent that only white children are children and also that only white people are actually intelligent this entire socialization concept is ridiculously fucked on so many levels that my own transmisogyny and internalized racism was really keeping me from seeing.]

5. it is interesting, is it not? how much clearer things become if we remove the 'trans' adjective from that statement. because it is clearly a factual error to say 'it doesn't seem fair to say that either men or women have it easier.' and, this, more than anything allows you to know that Teich is not operating within a framework wherein trans women are women and trans men are men. because the sentence 'it doesn't seem fair to say that either (trans) men or (trans) women have it easier' is glaringly wrong regardless of whether or not the 'trans' qualifier is used.

because I don't want to focus on proving that reality is, well, reality and that statements of fact are true. i want to focus on what white men like Teich have to gain by perpetuating the socialization myth. because it isn't accidental that a foundational, basic book like this was published. and was written by a white man. and that it presents a very specific white, male trans discourse on gender.

the socialization myth is one of the stronger weapons used against trans feminine people when we seek access to 'women's spaces'. this is also the myth that allows trans men to continue having access to women's only spaces.

of course, many people who aren't trans women tend to find this a trivial concern. sure. okay. except that when you spend even a moment thinking about it, it isn't trivial.

it is generally accepted that women face higher rates of sexual assault, rape, domestic violence, etc etc.

on every single one of these, trans women are much much much more at risk. this is, in part, because of other socio-economic factors. but it is nonetheless a reality. a matter of fact.

these two facts combine to make it such that most of the services provided for victims/survivors of rape, sexual assault, domestic violence are targeted and geared towards women. except that many of these places will not help trans women. but they do help trans men.

Teich's invocation of the socialization myth in this chapter (and in his larger discourse) supports this situation. The situation where the group of people who have the greatest need for a very limited amount of resources is precluded out of a massively transmisogynist notion that trans women were socialized as men.

So, yeah. sure. of course a white trans man would say that it isn't fair to say who has it worse. [6]

6. and I'm sure that there are more than a few different people recalling Audre Lorde's words about hierarchies of oppression right now... but if you are having this thought, you might want to think twice about applying it to a situation where Black trans women are demonstrably -- by any measure imaginable -- clearly more oppressed than any a trans man of any race. This also extends to Latina trans women, and to a lesser extent all trans feminine people of colour

another note...

do not allow the age of relationships to convince you that having people in your life who do not or cannot see you as a human being is somehow okay. it isn't.

expect and demand better.

a lot of people will suggest that you be 'patient' and give people time to adjust to the new ways that you are embodying and expressing your gender. it is okay to do this, so long as you have the energy and ability to. so long as you can do so safely and while prioritizing your own needs and health.

it is not wrong to expect that people treat you like a human being every single time they interact with you. That they use your name, your pronouns, etc. Every. Single. Time. That they respect your boundaries. Do not ask invasive questions. Do not make assumptions about your body and what you may or may not be planning to do with it.

The expectation that the people in your life treat you like a full, complex human being is the minimum.

which also means that you should be careful about praising people meeting this minimum standard of respect. otherwise, you run the risk of training them into behaviour that trades minimum standards for the loftiest goals. this is not the case. [7]

---

7. Fe -- it feels somewhat necessary to also say do not be ashamed if you do not feel safe enough to do this everytime or with everyone for survival purposes. it could fall back under that 'out' narrative.

4.2 Medically

Teich's book goes on to talk about hormones, surgeries, etc. This isn't something that I'm going to discuss a great deal since my general policy is:

whatever steps you feel are necessary to fully, comfortably, and happily embody your gender are good, necessary, and exactly what you should do

We could, however, discuss the medicalisation of gender and how this has created a situation where cis, often white doctors are the gatekeepers for access to necessary medical care. But, there is already a great deal written about this. About how the stringent, almost compulsory medical transition requirements for changing documentation create a situation where the most vulnerable people (trans feminine people of colour) are most often not only unable to access expensive medical care, but cannot get their documentation changed to accurately reflect their gender.

These are all supremely important issues. But, again, these issues are well known.

As far as decolonizing white trans/gender notions of medical transition goes, the clearer examples are those where we can see how the medicalisation of gender, and the nexus of issues surrounding it, is actually hegemonic. And it is also something often reinforced by white trans/gender discourse, in its almost obsessive focus on the body as the locus of gender.

Because we all well know that there are many, many, many examples of cultures that have gender systems that are not white. That do not, at a fundamental level, operate with a binary notion of gender. That there are indigenous genders beyond 'white man' and 'white woman'.

And the first, perhaps largest, problem with white trans/gender discourse is how it supports and participates in the pathologizing of indigenous genders. And it does so in a multiplicity of ways that are often quite subtle.

When I think about medical transition, it often makes me wonder. Since my bakla ancestors clearly weren't able to do HRT or SRS, and yet were able to function socially and spiritually as 'women' [1]. So what does it mean that we've come to a place where some bakla, in the Philippines, are using birth control as a means to access HRT? How much of this is, in part, a result of a white understanding that being a 'transgender woman' means HRT and SRS? What relation does it have to translating a medicalised white gender 'trans woman' for bakla, which in pre-colonial times, was a socio-spiritual identity?

And I don't ask these questions to suggest that, had these technologies been available 500 years ago, no bakla would use them. This is unknowable. Just as real is the sincere desire many bakla have to medically transition with either HRT or SRS (or both). What I think is that not much has actually changed. Some bakla are women. Some are femme gay men. Some are ladyboys (ie 'neither'). Some of us will want medical transition, some of us won't. I think that this diversity, this plurality has likely been a part of our community since the beginning.

Rather, I want to point to the process by which a medicalisation of gender shifts the focus from how a person's gender is embedded within a socio-spiritual community, to a function of their body. Another way to express this is to point out that it is a shift from 'gender roles' to 'gender'. It also instantiates a larger colonial notion that identity and being is primarily a 'private' and 'personal' affair. It dislocates people with indigenous genders from their socio-spiritual contexts and considers them as a singular unit. It fundamentally changes what it means to 'embody' your gender.

It also suggests that by operating on that singular unit, by operating on the body, that this is the means by which we become who we are. And, yes, this is exactly the process that facilitates our devaluation and dehumanization in our communities.

Because, at least in the case of the Philippines, this was about power. Shifting the focus onto our bodies is one of the steps that the spanish

1. 'women' is only in scare quotes here because of the ways that, from what I can tell, 'functioning as a women' for pre-colonial bakla people was not considered the equivalent as being a woman. As in, it was (possibly) understood to be a distinct identity, even as the social and spiritual roles were largely the same as a woman

took in order to begin subverting the structures that allowed Bakla to be spiritual aids to the women who were spiritual leaders. A dialectic of the trans feminine body as, since unalterable at those points, was based on notifying and convincing bakla that we were really just men. And by being 'men' we could have greater power and status within the catholic church than under the baybaylan.

fast forward to today, and we see that the medicalisation of gender is still about power. since we have a system that is set up to systematically privilege white women and white men over and above trans feminine people of colour. And, in doing so, because medical transition is necessary in most jurisdictions to have your identity documents change, gives them greater access to a host of other privileges granted to those people legitimized by the state.

and it is the compulsory and coercive nature of the medicalisation of gender that reveals its colonial and hegemonic intent. because outside of just Argentina, at present time, almost every single jurisdiction requires some level of medical intervention in order to obtain documents reflecting your gender (even if the medical intervention is just a letter from a doctor or therapist stating your gender, it is still an intervention that removes agency from the person to determine what their own gender is) [2].

It is, overall, a process by which we are stripped of our agency, humanity, and our right to self-determination. We must constantly seek validation from outside sources in order to be perceived as legitimate. It creates a sub-class of human being who are simply not allowed to just be.

---

2. note: i'm not including places like Pakistan, India, Bangladesh, and Nepal where it is possible to obtain documents as 'third gender' since the policies are somewhat different and it is unclear -- to me at least -- what the requirements are for getting this recognition. Moreover, while this may not be something that is being actively worked towards or even desired, it also does not appear that those individuals simply wanting an 'F' designation are allowed to do so. That they must either be 'M' or whatever the third gender category is. Argentina has a good law, since it gives maximum agency to individuals by allowing them 100% self-determination, with no outside intervention, for what their gender should be. However, they don't seem to allow for a third gender option, which -- at least in case of Nepal -- is explicitly what was desired. All of this to say: it is fucking complicated, okay? But, the ideal law would be, self-determination with more than two options.

5. the (white) history of transgenderism and its evolution (in modern times)

5.1 White american history

I honestly don't even quite know where to start with this chapter. I don't know how to address a statement as absurd as

> Endocrinologist Herry Benjamin is known as the 'founding father of contemporary western transsexualism." [1]

Teich literally does nothing to contextualize this statement. Doesn't talk about what it means for some cis white doctor to be the 'father of transsexualism'. Doesn't talk about the inherent colonialism of WPATH once being named after this doctor. Doesn't talk about how much harm and damage this one man has done to trans women.

Nothing. Just a quick biography of who Harry Benjamin was and what he did.

Well…

mr. Benjamin here is responsible, in many ways, for a lot of the problems and systemic discrimination that occurs around access for medical transition. He is, by his belief that being transgender was a medical problem, a great deal responsible for the medicalisation of gender.

But we shouldn't understand this as originating with him. It doesn't. Rather, he represents the culmination of a centuries long process that dislocated trans feminine people of colour from our communities through sustained focus (and control) on our bodies. The moment the first missionaries and explorers encountered us (wherever we may have been) and began examining our bodies to discover what we really were, mr. Benajmin was inevitable.

It was inevitable that a technology would be created to help some trans women better embody their gender, but that this technology, rather than simply existing to benefit us and improve our lives, would, instead, be used to control us. That it would ensure that any who so desired to improve our lives via medical transition would

1. Page 62, Teich, 2012, Transgender 101: A simple guide for a complex subject

have to sign up for, in some cases, a lifetime of medical and/or state surveillance. That in order to access these technologies you would have to make a bargain to give up autonomy, agency, and self-determination.

It was inevitable that this technology and the oppressive rules for accessing it would feed into a colonial entity like the World Professional Association of Transgender Health, since it originated in colonialism. And, lastly, it was inevitable that this technology, and the attendant gender system it reified, would further serve to destabilize IaoPoC gender systems the world over.

Actually...

You know what? Fuck Teich and his bullshit white mythology in this chapter.

I could write an entire book, on its own, for all the reasons why his 'history of transgenderism and evolution in modern times' is so full of lies, omissions, white supremacist garbage. From his white-washed account of the Stonewall Riots, to the tokenizing mention of We'wha. As well as the generalization of TDoR as being about 'transpeople' when it is really about trans feminine IaoPoC.

Moving on 'cause I just realized that I wasn't actually finished with the chapter...

5.2 the genesis of an imaginary community

While I don't want to use too many academic sources, there is one book that helps us understand how we got to where we are today, *Imagining Transgender: An Ethnography of a Category*. In it, the writer, David Valentine, examines:

> the recent (and spectacular) rise and institutionalization of transgender as a collective term to incorporate all and any variance from imagined gender norm [1]

We noted in chapter 2.1 that 'transgender' as a term representing a **community** is a fairly recent innovation and that its historical context reveals its hegemonic and imperialist goals. but this doesn't mean that the people putatively 'belonging' to this 'community' didn't exist prior to this usage (or to the colonial aspirations of white trans people). obviously we were here.

but part of the problem inherent in Valentine's book and other recountings of the history of transgender and/or the history of homosexuality, is that neither tends to account for the ways that **both** emerged as whites began to exert hegemonic control over (for lack of a better word) queer discourse. most histories will discuss how, for example, Sylvia Rivera (and other trans women of colour) was pushed out of the Gay Liberation Front by white gays as a means to divorce themselves from the disreputable ~trans women~ for a bid of respectability politics.

of course, it worked, given that the GLF was able to obtain some sort of civil recognition while entirely ommitting the needs of trans women from it. and it is something that continues to impact queer organizing in the usa, since more recently we see that in trying to aim for non-discriminatory legislation, white gays again are willing to remove more 'controversial' trans inclusive sections in order to obtain their own rights.

---

1. David Valentine, *Imagining Transgender: An Ethnography of a Category* (Durham: Duke University Press, 2007), 14.

"Transgender" in this collective sense, then, arose in the United States in uneven, often contested ways, primarily in white, middle-class activist contexts in New York and California in the 1990s [2]

on the otherside, we see explications from books like Valentine's (and other places) that discuss the rise of transgender activism in the 90s (coinciding with the emergence of the umbrella use of 'transgender'), can even note the interlacing aspect of race and class, but fail to understand in many ways how this is a historical enactment of a hegelian type of dialectic[3].

however, while one might be inclined to think of the white gay movement as the thesis, the white trans movement as the antithesis, and the eventual integration of the communities (which is, let us be super clear, a real and apparent goal of many people from both communities) is the desired synthesis.

except, this would be wrong. this historical narrative is white mythology.

we can see this from Valentine's introductory comments on his book. when he muses that his project was intended to be one thing, but became another because of his interactions with trans women of colour:

"I've been gay all my life, been a woman all my life," says Fiona. I am sitting with Fiona and five other people…two of us…identify as [cis] gay men and are white, male-bodied, middle-class professionals. The other five, including Fiona, though born male, present themselves and live their lives as feminine people and are either African American or Latina.

However, although the group is billed as a transgender support group, none of the participants routinely refer to themselves as transgender. More often, they talk about

2. David Valentine, *Imagining Transgender: An Ethnography of a Category* (Durham: Duke University Press, 2007), 33.

3. Hegelian dialectic = thesis, antithesis, and then synthesis

themsevles as girls, sometimes as fem queens, every now
and then as women, but also very often as gay.[4]

This book was written in 2007. Which is not so very long ago. Given
that **both** the gay whites and trans whites have been pushing a
party line that makes a strong distinction between 'sexuality' and
'gender,' it seems almost unbelievable that this poor, mistaken
women would be making such ontological/categorical mistakes.

obviously, if you are ~male bodied~ but live as a 'feminine person,'
you are trans, not gay.

when we put this into context of the GLF pushing Sylvia Rivera out
(and Marsha P. Johnson), many things become clear:

- trans feminine people of colour started stonewall (Marsha
  P. Johnson literally threw the first stone), which is still
  considered the defining moment in modern history for the
  beginning of the 'gay' movement
- mere years later, these same people are systematically
  pushed out of the movement they started and subsequently
  erased from history
- white trans ppl do nothing
- a little while later, trans whites realize they've been
  screwed over and that trans women of colour are starting
  to do things again
- thus, the 'transgender community' is created by white,
  middle-class trans people who, rather than oppose, actually
  compliment the white gay movement.
- however, it remains important to both white movements to
  maintain an appearance of opposition as a means to
  prevent trans women of colour from organizing or retaking
  the movements we began and to continue to exploit our
  labour, our deaths, and our lives.

The point being, **both** communities exist to enforce and reinforce
a white hegemonic conception of gender and sexuality. and, in the
ways that these movements have become global, this hegemonic
force isn't just about gate keeping to the communities, but also about
continuing hundreds of years of colonizing iaopoc genders and
peoples.

4. David Valentine, *Imagining Transgender: An Ethnography of a Category* (Durham:
Duke University Press, 2007), 18.

it is a strange process of white people initially via colonial structures, coming to pathologize, criminalize, and eradicate iaopoc genders and sexualities in order to enforce a white patriarchy and binary

and then, to prevent real change via decolonization, co-opting and stealing a movement with revolutionary power into selling a brand of freedom that requires buying into white supremacy in order to be viable.

and so, nothing changes. white supremacy and colonialism rules the day. white gays and trans whites take their rightful place amongst white supremacy and trans women of colour continue to be violently targeted because our continued existence will always destablize and challenge white supremacy. it is why we cannot be allowed to exist.

and trans whites have no more desire to ensure our freedom from oppression than do white gays or white ppl in general.

5.3 some thoughts on history

However, I do have some general comments I'd like to make about the history of 'transgender' in a global setting. Given what the world is today and the continuing echoes and reverberations of colonialism, some of us may not actually have access to our cultural heritage and histories. Many of us live in the diaspora. And even those that don't live in the diaspora, white colonialism has done a very excellent job of erasing or rewriting our histories in many areas of the world.

(The Philippines, for example, what bakla are now and what we once were are so wildly divergent that even though I know my own heritage, it still requires considerable effort to access the actual history of my gender, rather than the white lies.)

And, I do have in mind one particular group of people: Black americans. The descendants of enslaved people (who, of course, are not limited to just Black americans).

The atlantic slave trade was horrific in pretty much all the ways imaginable. It also had the very clear effect of dislocating a huge population of people from their original cultures and heritages. Now, many hundreds of years later, many descendants of enslaved Africans have no way of accessing this heritage. They have, however, created unique and vibrant cultures of their own.

For all that there are barriers to accessing my own heritage (linguistic, geographic, etc.), I do have, at least the benefit of knowing pretty much exactly where my people came from (Pasay City). Not all IaoPoC have that.

And so, yes, I claim my gender as traditional, but not in a way that is... shall we say nostalgic or as part of a way to establish my gender as more legitimate than anyone else's. Perhaps one of the bitterest pills to swallow about decolonizing is the knowing that we will not get anywhere if we attempt to recreate the past. We cannot reverse time and go back to what we once were[1].

When you heal a wound, it often leaves a scar. The healing has happened but nothing is the same.

Also. Putting forward an understanding that IaoPoC genders must all be 'traditional' in order to be legitimate, does a great deal of harm to all the diasporic communities that have continued to find creative and powerful ways to resist colonization, while in the belly of the beast.

What I'm trying to say here is that something like ball culture, which is modern and must, in part, be understood within the context that it arose, which means partially informed by white gender systems. And that we must understand that this site of resistance to white gender normativity is equally important in seeing our way to true decolonization as understanding 'traditional' indigenous genders. As in, modern responses and sites of resistance are needed just as much as recovering our traditional knowledges.

Also important are the ways that various IaoPoC cultures today are strategically using elements of white trans/gender discourse to empower themselves and actually overcome earlier colonial holdouts that have entrenched transmisogynist oppression in their cultures. By this I mean several of the areas in South Asia mobilizing and using the 'third gender' notion to obtain documentation and recognition within their legal/cultural frameworks. Like Pakistan recently had a few transgenders run for political office, something that was only possible after they received state recognition as a third gender[2].

All of this to say, that we have made our own history. And we continue to make our own history.

---

1. and possibly, there are many good arguments why this would be undesirable. since, it would be a very big mistake to assume that all pre-colonial cultures were magically free of oppression. not only would this be demonstrably false, but it also serves to reify white supremacist notions about indigenous peoples by not understanding IaoPoC cultures and civilizations as equally complex as white cultures. Things were different but different doesn't necessarily mean better.

2. 'third gender' of course being a white supremacist framework for understanding the multitude of IaoPoC genders, as well as non-consensual third gendering being very frequently used to de-legitimize the status of trans women as women

Decolonizing trans/gender histories must account both for what we once were and who we are today. This means grappling with the harm done to us by colonialism and healing it. It requires not reviving the past, but moving forward. It involves not only understanding what we can learn from our traditions and knowledge, but seeing the plurality of modern resistance to white trans/gender colonialism happening the world over. [3]Fe -- it occurred to me that white people are so used to using and rewriting history for their own purposes that they erase their ability to be full beings in their quest to eradicate IaoPoc, and especially those affected by transmisogyny.[4]

3.

4.

6. the pathology of being transgender

6.1 The colonial origins of Transgender Pathology

Teich and many others usually begin their histories of the pathologization and/or medicalisation of trans/gender with white ppl and the start of sexology sometime around the mid-to-late 1800s. But the origins of prurient, cis interest in the genitals and physiology of trans feminine ppl started much, much earlier. And it did not start in white countries focused on white bodies.

Rather, it started in the colonies. It started when white ppl began to interact with Indigenous ppls with different gender systems. Some of these gender systems allowed for more variation and pluralism of gender than they were really able to comprehend. Or understand.

And so began around 500 years of cis pre-occupation with the genitals of trans women and/or trans feminine ppl. Coincidentally (I'm sure) this is also the beginning of transmisogyny and the gender binary. Both tools of colonialism, of genocide, of settlement, of empire. [1]

These histories of transmisogyny also make it quite clear just why there is no 'transphobia', only transmisogyny. There is and has been a vast erasure of the trans masculine or of trans men from the histories. And while this is, of course, tragic, the jealousy and pettiness of trans men over the hypervisibility that resulted from

1. nica -- also, to draw or connect this to antiblackness--settlement in the 'New World' was enabled by slavery, funded by it (search Tyron P. Woods on my blog for a quote I recently posted, if interested), that black bodies were a part of settlement, property expansion, and that the gender binary, as a system meant to instill the humanity of white settlers, required, alongside the genocidal coercion of indigenous peoples into white settler categories, that blackness only be granted 'gender' insofar as it meant reproduction of property. or that the white binary is as much about settler society as it is about blackness as non-human, absolutely incapable of containing or having gender- instead, of being 'contained' by it -- this is the intervention on 'gender' made by Black woman theorists Hortense Spillers, Saidiya Hartman and Tiffany King (whom u can also search on my blog)---- so the gender binary as connected to white humanity is also upheld by the absolute irrelevance of gender on black bodies, with exception to the reproduction of property ... not to mention the violent torture focused on the genitals of enslaved/captive Black ppl, another preoccupation w genitals

this white (and soon to be cis) gaze on our bodies is, well, also transmisogyny. As is equivocating erasure with violent suppression, surveillance, violation experienced by trans women of colour at the hands of white settlers and colonialists for hundreds of years. [2]

And this is a pattern that continues to this very day. And we can see, also coincidentally, I'm sure, that the vast majority of the deaths of TWoC and trans feminine PoC occurs on settled lands and former colonial territories. Often in areas where, if you dig into the early or pre-colonial history, have Indigenous ppls with historical gender systems that had space and respect enough for #girlslikeus, to not attempt a systematic and total eradication of our existence — whatever our place in the respective culture.

> Neither Alcina nor the author of the earlier 'Manila Manuscript' arrived at this latter point immediately, but it seemed to develop through a process of elimination, as they sought to discover any deficiencies or difference in the sexual anatomy of the asog that might explain why a male would voluntarily reject his masculinity (which in Spanish codes equated with privilege) and identify as a woman. Alcina and the author of the 'Manila Manuscript' were unanimous in their opinion that 'almost all asog are impotent for the reproductive act,' and therefore 'deficient for the practice of matrimony.' Alcina's curiosity regarding the 'deficient' genitals of the asog remained unfulfilled, since he admitted that the 'mute indian,' 'would never allow himself to be touched, nor would he ever bathe in front of others.' [3]

2. Fe -- should it also be mentioned that fluid and variant waf who are not trans men contribute to this here? that instead of discussing how that erasure limits our ability to conceive ourselves we very willingly enforce transmisogyny or is the focus on trans men here only due to Teich's agenda?

3. nica -- the last comment i wrote, on antiblackness & slavery, was made before reading this paragraph. but i would say that in both instances genitals relate to the in/capacity (the violent 'emasculation' of Black men/rape of Black women) of reproducing property -- though, of course, since the aims of genocide and slavery, operate on different blood logics, 'indigenous' blood as always disappearing and 'blackness' as expansive under the one-drop rule, the problem located on the 'male' person 'incapable' of matrimony is tied to 'his' failure to amalgamate into white settler society while the category of 'female' again means rape while Black men are emasculated due to the master's need to destroy kinship ties among captive communities, imposing patriarchal understanding of kinship here -- hopefully this

> However, presumably to satiate his curiosity, Alcina persisted in his search for an anatomical answer. He attempted to discover whether the asog constituted a third hermaphroditically-sexed group; that is a group possessing both male and female reproductive organs. In this pursuit, he abandoned his efforts to surreptitiously view the genitals of his subject and turned instead for information to other members of the community who were surprisingly forthcoming in their disavowal of the existence of hermaphrodites. However, Alcina was reluctant to believe them, instead suggesting that 'these matters ... are verified with difficulty' — and verification was what he lacked.[4]

As we can see here, the very heart of the medicalisation of gender is biological essentialism. These spanish colonialists literally were incapable of comprehending the existence of bayog or asog without reducing us to our bodies. Without speculating on our genitals. Without explicitly seeking to violate our consent with their white gaze. Our existence is incomprehensible within the spanish binarist and patriarchal gender system, since to exist is to be giving up a place of privilege (one that didn't exist prior to their arrival).

This, of course, is only **one** example of this. This fascination and desire to lay bare our bodies to the white gaze can be seen wherever colonialists encountered individuals whose existence was likewise incomprehensible.

Thus. We can see that here in the origins of transmisogyny and the binary, trans/gender has always been pathologized and medicalised. It was, at first contact, the way that our bodies were rendered inert and inhuman, as objects of study for white ppl. When we became dehumanized and deviant.

makes sense. and again, these come to mind because of the connection between gender and settlement/genocide as also dependent on/enabled by antiblackness | so, I should have searched 'asog' before writing the last comment - the context of asog became clear to me in the next two paragraphs- my comment may be (?) applicable to how property and indigeneity (its elimination) work in the Philippines

4. Brewer, Carolyn. "Intersections: Baylans, Asogs, Transvestism, and Sodomy: Gender, Sexuality and the Sacred in Early Colonial Philippines." Intersections: Gender, History and Culture in the Asian Context no. 2 (1999). http://intersections.anu.edu.au/issue2/carolyn2.html.

A history that only continues when we view how modern trans/ gender medicine developed with ppl like Hirschfiel and Benjamin[5]. Who largely remained focused on trans women's bodies and, later, on our minds/psychology. That we came to drive a mental disorder into the DSM is only the culmination of something that had been going on for centuries.

And the application of this process/machinery/institution has only recently been applied to trans men. The history of the medicalization and pathologisation of trans/gender is also the history of transmisogyny and the violation of non-white body by colonialists. They are all things intimately entwined and connected, such that attempting to speak of things like biological gender essentialism is impossible without understanding how this was mobilized to dislocate iaopoc trans feminine ppl from our communities and enforce a patriarchy would eliminate us and oppress the 'real' women.

5. For people wanting a good history on this, I recommend: D'orsay, Toni. Introduction to Transness - Complete. Accessed August 20, 2013. http://www.dyssonance.com/wp-content/uploads/2013/08/Introduction-to-Transness.pdf.

6.2 Fe/male socialization

6.2.1 Initial thoughts

Been seeing a lot recently about the supposed male socialization of trans women... both from cis ppl and trans women. This is my contribution for why it is incoherent and just a silencing and oppressive and transmisogynist tool.

Firs... there is this notion that children, depending on assigned sex, get one message about gender stuff and not the other. This is largely nonsensical. We all get the exact **same** message. Because ideas and oppression don't exist in isolation. For the most part, the message boils down to (if'n we're talking just about gender):

Boys rule and girls drool.

Or something to that effect. Both boys and girls are socialized to behave as if this were true. It isn't that boys are taught that girls are subservient and that girls are taught to defer to boys. Well, yes, we are taught that, but these are behavioural patterns designed to inculcate all genders with the same message. Children of all genders are socialized to behave in ways that assume only two genders and that one of those genders (girls) is worth far less than the other gender.

So. If we are all getting the same message, how to make sense of the differences between how one child embodies this message and how another does? Well, largely based on which gender they are told they are mixed with whatever gender they actually are. Outside of the rare moments where you are explicitly and on an individual basis told the message, most of the time we sort of... just pick this up from our peers, how our parents interact with one another, what we see on tv, what we read in books, etc.

And that is the thing. We all watch (within certain variations) the same shows. Read the same books. Because, um, you know, we all lived in the same culture (obvs. relative to geography but I'm working on a really macro basis rn).

It blows my mind that all these feminist media critics or whatever can spend their lives deconstructing the harmful messages encoded in many of our cultural products and practices and somehow think that trans girls didn't internalize and embody these things as well.

For example. Just on the impossible standards of beauty alone. We hear a lot from cis women who talk about how this impossible ideal beauty destroys confidence and self-worth and self-esteem, but can't quite make the leap to how this impacts trans girls.

We see the same impossible ideal of beauty. And I'm not sure if you've realized (although, since many of you take exquisite pleasure in de/misgendering us, i'm sure you _do_ realize), just how distant that ideal is for your average trans woman. Especially if you transition late. Many of us understand that even if we go through the entire gamut of surgeries/hormones/whatever we will **never** be beautiful. We will never be desirable. We will never be attractive. And, the thing is, this isn't a newborn realization.

Why? Becasuse we've been exposed to and socialized with the **exact same** impossible beauty standards that cis women were. Because. You know, we share the same cultural and were likewise socialized **together**.

There is no 'male socialization' and no 'female socialization'. We are all just socialized in a culture that devalues and oppresses women. And these social behaviours are supported and rewarded and enforced by our institutions.

6.2.2 Further thoughts

After posting the previous section on my blog, I got into a discussion on FB with another trans girl about whether or not, um, the general message is tailored depending on how people perceive you and/or based on your assigned sex/gender.

I asked this question in an ask i got about this:

> What is the difference between a five year old girl being told to talk softly and defer to boys and a twenty-five year old woman being told the same thing?

The response she gave was that as an adult, she has the ability to resist this message and a lifetime of habit thinking that this 'defer to boys' notion doesn't apply to her. I'm not going to say anything about the latter half of the statement since this is her experience and okay.

I do take some issue with the first half because girls of any and all ages do resist this and all other messages that tell us we are worthless. We may not resist it entirely (impossible in this system) or even with great success (depending on your personal context the punishment for resistance can be mild or severe).

I don't necessarily disagree that how other people treat you based on their erroneous perception or understanding of your gender has a profound impact on your developed behaviour/attitude.

I guess what I'm not understanding is how, if we are to label this sub-section of our experiences (ie, other people's perception of us) as 'male socialization', but not the general cultural messages we all internalize....

Then in a singular sense we most certainly cannot talk about 'male socialization' or 'female socialization' as things that exist. We can only talk about 'male socialization**s**' and 'female socialization**s**'. For if we take the multiplicity of identity seriously, as we must, then we are socialized as a whole person based on the nexus of the parts of our identity and our axes of oppression.

Because it is incoherent, on this notion of socialization (or any i suspect) to assert that Asian girls are socialized in exactly the same way as white girls (all other things being equal). And it only gets more complex once we factor in all other aspects and considerations.

Indeed, it gets complex enough that we could assert, easily, that each individual is socialized in unique ways that cannot be assumed true of any other person, since no one else shares our **exact** context. Not even my sister was socialized in the same way that I was[1].

---

1. And I stg if anyone makes this about gender i'll punch you. For pin@y families, the difference of birth order between my ate and I entails different socialization, since she had different expectations/messages because she was first born.

Because using the example above, how do we reconcile that 'girls should be quiet and defer' with the 'angry' stereotype that Black (and girls) often have to navigate?

This possibility of individual specific socialization is why I chose to speak at the macro level. Since, to use my circular room/pot metaphor[2], even the individuals side by side, with considerable overlap, are still seeing a slightly different angle of the pot.

But in aggregate the pot (ie, message) that girls are worthless and men gold, is what we are all looking at.

And I guess both my fb interlocutor and i are guilty of the same error of generalizing our invidual experiences. Since, to some extent, I don't see 'male socialization' as something that occurred in large quantities in my life partly based on my family/race situation and because, even as an Asian perceived boy, many of the so-called 'male behaviours' were not something I was raised to embody, particularly not in a culture that consistently emasculates and/or feminizes Asian men/boys. I can see how a white person probably had a very different experience.

In any case, the macro message remains the same. And it is still an error to speak of 'female/male socialization' as if it were one monolithic experience.

2. b. binaohan. Oh, the hu-manatee. Nov 3, 2013. http://b-binaohan.tumblr.com/post/65889617756

7. discrimination

7.1 The Pervasive Culture of Transmisogyny (and cissexism, i guess)

So Teich's major point in the first section is that cissexism is entrenched in our cultures. Such that a lot of cis people feel 100% comfortable asking invasive, dehumanizing questions. Okay. Sure. Of course, this book is being written by me, which means that I'm going to talk more about transmisogyny.

In part because one of the damaging aspects of this chapter is that Teich is operating with some notion that there is a general sort of discrimination experienced by the 'trans community'. Which is, to be super clear, a fucking lie. And it is a lie perpetuated by white trans men like him because it helps them. It helps them write books like this, as if he were able to actually comment on the lives and oppression experienced by trans feminine iaopoc.

He creates this equivalence by alternating between talking about trans men and talking about trans women. Acting as if men and women, by the magical virtue of being trans, suddenly have a shared experience that cis men and cis women are never assumed to have.

However, this isn't simply a value-neutral oversight without consequence. Something revealed in one of the later paragraphs:

> What about a transman who needs to seek respite in a shelter for those affected by domestic violence? Most of those shelters are for women only. If any are available for men, and again the person is pre-op or non-op, then he may be rejected from all sides. It is true that many women may feel threatened by the presence of a man in such a shelter. But how can this transman's needs be met? [1]

Okay? If you can't see why this hypothetical situation is massively transmisogynist and, essentially bullshit, then... well. i don't know what to say.

1. Teich (2012) page 99

Teich writes this despite the vast evidence that, by and large, most cases of trans 'people' being turned away for services intended for women (homeless shelters, rape crisis centres, domestic violence shelters, etc etc etc) are, in fact, trans women, not trans men.

Who gives a flying fuck what about teh tranz menz? Most, if not all, of these men enjoy unrestricted access to women's spaces that often will bar trans women because 'it is true that many women may feel threatened by the presence of a man in such a shelter' [2].

It is a very tangible example of the ways that trans men and trans women experience cissexist discrimination and oppression in fundamentally different ways. Because Teich has to pose a hypothetical situation here. But I can think of, off the top of my head, one example from this year (2013) where an organisation released a report about homeless trans women being barred from shelters. Or, in a super famous case, where a rape crisis centre was supported in firing a trans women (and is supported in having an explicit policy discriminating against trans women). And both of these examples are from super duper progressive canada, in two of the super duper progressive cities.

No hypotheticals are needed to show how transmisogynist discrimination directly impacts the lives of trans women in ways that are simply unknown to trans men.

one side comment, concerning Teich's unbelievably ridiculous assertion that children are more likely to be accepting of a person being trans. he makes this claim with reference to absolutely zero evidence or any perceptible relation to reality.

he notes, on the one hand, that gender policing begins at a young age. but children have had less time to absorb this indoctrination.

okay… but no. Not only is this condescending, but it entirely removes from the fact that children are often some of the most effective gender policemen of other children. That it is their teasing and bullying — resulting from receiving transmisogynist messages all their life — is actually one of the most potent ways that gender

---

2. Teich (2012) page 99

is policed and how we come to understand and internalize transmisogyny.

because the pressure we feel from our peers and the human need to socialize and belong, means that we usually start, at a very young age, to conform to gender norms to avoid being outcast. Teich, of course, is focused on how children can (allegedly) be more accepting of an adult's transition. but nowhere does he address how accepting (or not) children are of their trans peers. why? because it is a big fucking problem that would entirely disarm his absurd point about 'innocent' children, as if they weren't already feeling and experiencing and expressing the full power of oppression. [3]

3. Fe -- Yes, that peer point is majorly important. This guy is completely failing to understand that children might accept him because as an adult his has more power and authority over them? of course he doesn't seem to really understand hierarchies of oppression, or at least he's pretending not to.

7.2 Anti-discrimination laws

This is probably going to be one of the areas where the decolonization aspect of this book is really easy to perceive. like. Teich makes an explicit claim that laws are a good way to ensure the safety of transpeople (99), while essentially contradiction himself on the next page by noting that often law enforcement is part of the discriminatory system that oppresses 'transpeople' (100).

Okay. Let me tell you why this is bullshit:

- laws might give some people recourse to address injustice, but this will often not be the people who need the most protection, since those people (and by 'people' i mean trans feminine iaopoc) often have the least access to the necessary resources to assert their rights. (ie. finding a lawyer, even having enough educational attainment to know they have applicable rights, time, energy, etc.).
- Laws do nothing about addressing the underlying attitudes and prejudices that cause discrimination in the first place, they only (hope) to serve as a costly deterrent from preventing people from overt expressions of discrimination. As any iaopoc knows, there are a 1000 and 1 different ways for covert discrimination to operate and circumvent discrimination laws.
- even more importantly (if we are talking about states like the usa or canada) looking to the state to stop oppressing its citizens, when those states literally exist as oppressive settler states that are illegitimately governing on stolen land, is so counter-intuitive that it is like when people blame seals for the collapse of fish stock in canada, but coming up with the solution that they should simply ask the seals to stop eating fish for the next 200 years in the hopes that the entirely destroyed ecosystem will fix itself.

That last point is crucial. Since the only thing I want from this state (being in canada) is for it to be dismantled and the land and resources it currently controls be immediately turned over to the First Nations currently being colonized and settled by this white supremacist settler state.

Literally the only thing that this government could do that might actually have the desired impact of reducing the oppression of trans feminine iaopoc would be to abdicate its false claims of sovereignty and dissolve itself. [1]

If we want a way forward that will actually work to reduce oppression, then the solution is complete and immediate decolonization. Now. Not tomorrow. Not after this government takes time to make a 'switch over' plan. Now. [2]

1. Fe -- I guess this would work if the goal was only to end the government's involvement, since our minds have been fucked enough that too many of us would be perfectly willing to replicate this, but yeah?.

2. Fe -- oh, well, yes, then. Reduce. Cue embarrassment, for not reading just two more lines.

7.3 Trans bathroom panic

This is easily the most ridiculous thing in the world and it is sad that it has such a major impact on the lives of any trans feminine iaopoc doing HRT (since most anti-androgens are diuretics). Thus, leaving us with a very real medical reason to pee a lot... but without much public access to restrooms.

So i don't want to diminish the importance of public accommodations, since these sorts of protections are massively important. But there is already a great deal about this issue, and discussing the issue doesn't really fulfill this books mission to decolonize trans 101.

when you look through this entire chapter on discrimination, you may notice two glaring omissions: violence and sex work.

instead, we have an entire section on the ways that trans bathroom panic is mobilized by transmisogynist shitheads to derail and re-frame the issue of public accommodation.

But in this same section, Teich again enacts transmisogyny by generalizing what trans bathroom panic is really about. And it isn't about trans men. No one is particularly worried about trans men using the appropriate washroom.

They are, however, very very very worried about 'men in dresses' using the appropriate washroom/change room/etc. to prey on 'women' or 'little girls'.

when, of course, we know that the opposite is true and that many trans women have been assaulted in public restrooms/changerooms/ etc. And that even in the rare cases that a trans woman is supported by an institution in accessing public spaces, it will become fodder for a media feeding frenzy.

Additionally, as noted in section 7.1, bathrooms — despite the continued fear they invoke in many transmisogynists imaginations — aren't even the most important public accommodations issues.

Stuff like access to homeless shelters or victim services are just as important, if not more so.

Then again, this is exactly why our attention is constantly drawn by transmisogynists to washrooms. Because, in comparison, it seems trivial but is incendiary enough that it can make headlines, because these same transmisogynist would much rather focus on hypothetical situations than deal with the reality they've created and are supporting that directly leads to the great amount of violence and oppression that trans women of colour have to deal with everyday.

because it isn't about fucking washrooms.

7.4 Family

I don't have too much to say about families, per se, since by and large, I agree with Teich's overall point that trans women face serious legal challenges when it comes to maintaining our families (re: if you've had kids, are married, etc.). In some countries simply transitioning will cause the state to dissolve your marriage (Italy's supreme court is currently deciding on this at the time of writing). It can complicate widow's benefits, inheritance, medical care (for people who may not be able to make their own decisions), and whole host of other issues relating to family law and relationships.

What does fascinate me, however, is the fact that of all the legal and justice discrimination faced by trans feminine iaopoc, this is what he chooses?

Not a single mention of unfair sentencing, of the struggles incarcerated #girlslikeus have (at least in the usa, where he is writing) in access appropriate and constitutionally guaranteed medical care, the reality that women are in men's prisons, that in some areas a trans woman carrying a condom can be charged with solicitation?

Nothing? Nope?

It is probably because most of these problems are issues that trans feminine iaopoc have to deal with and that white trans men like Teich, rarely do. Because, maybe for him, the worst legal discrimination he can think of relates to custody and family law (which, yeah, not diminishing the importance of this at all but IT IS THE ONLY THING HE MENTIONS IN THE SECTION ON LEGAL DISCRIMINATION — which unduly elevates its importance).

Or, re: decolonizing. No mentions of the legal discrimination when it comes to trans women seeking to be refugees. Or even just trans feminine iaopoc having serious problems navigating the transmisogynist immigration system.

Or, for fuck's sake, the problems with obtaining documentation matching your gender? Like, even as a trans man, he must have *some* opinion about the widespread (and global) problems that trans people have with this?

All of this aggregates to a situation where bullshit trans 101s like this render invisible and contribute to the struggles and oppression that trans feminine iaopoc have to deal with because it focuses only on the problems that the most privileged within the community are likely to have, rather than focusing on the problems of the least privileged.

7.5 Bullying and trans kids

I can't deal with this section. Because all he does is, more or less, talk about slurs and cite some figures on how trans children feel unsafe in school. Okay.

But no connections to the stuff he discusses in the rest of the chapter. Or how living in a society with institutionalized transmisogyny means that these children are supported in their 'bullying' (re: oppressive hegemonic actions) by their teachers? Who also participate in creating this same culture by implicitly permitting or by being one of the active contributors?

Notice how the focus in this section is on the individual children and their feelings. They feel unsafe at school. Okay. This is, without a doubt, not a good thing. But what is the point of making this claim without making the related claim that they feel unsafe at school, because it is unsafe for them. That they are at constant risk from anything from microaggressive shit to outright violence and assault?

I also note that he makes no mention of race. Because the NTDS report Injustice at Every Turn[1], has an interesting note that iaopoc and/or poor people were more likely to express gender non-conformity at school[2]. This means, that the children experiencing a great deal of this bullying are poor iaopoc (let us not even pretend for a moment that there is no significant overlap between class and race). And of these children, given the reality of transmisogyny, it is most often trans feminine iaopoc girls.

In a lot of ways... the myths that he is trading on to build his comments in this section are amongst the grossest because this myth of a coherent trans community whose issues are the same and whose gendered experiences are the same, simply serves to whitewash and masc-wash(?) the actual issues at hand.

1. Grant, Jaime M., Lisa A. Mottet, Justin Tanis, Jack Harrison, Jody L. Herman, and Mara Keisling. Injustice at Every Turn: A Report of the National Transgender Discrimination Survey. Washington: National Center for Transgender Equality and National Gay and Lesbian Task Force, 2011.
2. Grant et al. 2011. 34.

Which allows him to write a three paragraph section on the experience of trans youth as if bullying (in the form of teasing) is the largest factor that leads trans feminine iaopoc to feel unsafe at school.

Worse, is the ways that there is little awareness of the ways that the institutionalized transmisogyny in schools is directly connected to every other institutional expression of transmisogyny. That this is the exact place where white and/or cis kids learn that trans feminine iaopoc have no worth and that there is literally no one (not teachers, not other students, no one) who will protect us from their cruelty.

7.6 Religion

The section Teich has on religion is… long but very light on any real discussion of the relevant issues. Or, for that matter, any issues at all. Just a few comments about how some christians will misuse the bible to excuse their oppressive attitudes and behaviours.

From a historical and colonial perspective, there is a great deal more to say about the transmisogynist history of christianity and missionaries. Because, in a few different places, transmisogyny was absolutely a necessary part of the colonial project and missionaries played a great role in institutionalizing transmisogyny.

Part of this is a simple result of the fact that there was not even an attempt to separate the church from the state, at the dawn of the colonial age, these two things were inextricably tied together. This has largely remained true for the entire history of the main colonial powers. as in, the start of the modern period and the sort of collapse of the major colonial powers from the world wars and the secularization that occurred happened after more than a few colonies gained independence).

It still remains true in the many settler states that pay lip service to a separation between church and state but, accidentally i'm sure, often use christian morals and values in their laws, or retain these values through an unwillingness to update old laws. or just because all settler states have a vested interest in maintaining their colonial/settler power and religion has always played a significant role in it. and we've just reached a moment in history where the influence of religion has been sublimated out of a desire to legitimize settler states as being more benevolent and progressive than they actually are (and, by default, more benevolent and progressive than any Indigenous form of governance since Indigenous peoples are always bound by their superstitions and mystic religions).

I mention all of this because it is important to understand that christian transmisogyny was actually born in the colonies and after their exposure to trans feminine people who often (but not always) had some kind of religious role in their communities.

and of course the desire was two-fold in this cases, dislocate the women from spiritual roles and the power inherent in them, as a necessary means to establishing their own power. and, in conjunction with this, focus on instituting a white hetero-patriarchal cis binary gender system, such that the priests and missionaries could establish and legitimize the political (and, remember the 'political' should not be understood as exclusive from the religious) power of the colonizer and/or the settler.

transmisogyny was a necessary part of colonialism exerting its hegemonic power over colonies. and this, of course, is also connected to the forced spread of christianity across the globe.

and it is often the remnants of christianity, or as is the case in many colonies the still living tradition, that is responsible for the existence of violent and virulent transmisogyny in areas that traditionally had trans feminine people as integral parts to their communities (and in places where trans feminine people are still integral parts of their communities).[1]

looked from a different angle... one could see that transmisogyny is inherent in any christian denomination that proselytizes (and thus is imperialist). because the white cisheteropatriarchal gender system is somewhat necessary for them to maintain hegemonic control over populations. it is, one might say, one of the tools they've learned works, and so they keep applying it to certain problems (with, as we can see from the current state of transmisogyny, great effect).

---

1. and, yes, with this later comment i definitely have in mind a place like Samoa where the fa'afafine still have an integral part in the community but that only just in 2013 decriminalized 'impersonating a woman' and is almost 100% christian

7.7 Passing

This is sort of a hotly contested notion in the trans 'community'. And there are many layers to it. Toni D'orsay, however, manages to succinctly cover the major points:

> 'Passing', as a concept, means "to be mistaken for something you are not'. That's the purpose of the notion, the nature of the idea, and the function of the term in language.
>
> In this case, "passing' means to be mistaken for a girl, when one "really isn't'. That's built into the term, the idea, and when people place that as a goal, as an aspiration or ideal, what they are saying is that they want to be mistaken by other people for something they are not.
>
> There is reason that it has this meaning, this purpose. That reason goes back a very long time, but the source of it comes from the street, like much within the trans community. In this case, however, it wasn't merely the street for trans folk, but the street as in the poorest parts of a given area or city. It is a very, very western term, adopted broadly, and the source for this term is people like myself.
>
> Light skinned black people.
>
> We pass for white. Being able to do that gives us access that people with darker shade tones do not have in a society that is hellbent on destroying people who's skin color is dark.[1]

The history of the term 'passing' is, as mentioned, located within the racial politics of the Black community. This is something that is critical to remember when the community is discussing 'passing' as a woman. Since, on the first pass, it seems to be appropriation in a very broad sense.

1. Toni D'orsay. http://tonidorsay.tumblr.com/post/55995980361/ciscritical-not cisphobic-sapphisms-replied-to

And ideological appropriation matters. Why? For this exact reason. Because the way that the trans community has taken a term that has a specific use and historical context has diluted the meaning and obscured it's actual meaning.

Passing means to pretend to be something you are not and, as D'orsay points out, it is nothing less than assimilation. Which, yes, I do get that there are many #girlslikeus that seek to assimilate into cis society. This isn't what I'm talking about. And this is why racial terms and gender terms don't have much overlap. If a iaopoc is light skinned enough to pass as white, then they are passing as something they are not (ie, white).

Trans women cannot pass as women. Trans women are women. And not even women with a different kind of history. Women aren't a monolith, there is no shared, universal experience of womanhood. You cannot pass as something you, in fact, actually are.

Other terms I've seen to replace passing (amongst people who know the history of the term) is 'blending' or 'stealth' or 'read'.

The term anyone uses isn't necessarily the most important or critical (aside from the appropriative 'passing'). What is important is the notion that some people who, by a number of overlapping privileges, are able to meet the fairly high standards required to appear like a white/able/thin/cis woman, choose not to disclose their entire medical history to everyone they meet. Some people in a similar boat (ie, capable of appearing like a white/able/thin/cis woman) choose to disclose their history.

Now, it is fairly well established that the more axes of oppression you face (particularly those centred around your body), the less likely it is people will regularly read you as a cis woman. On this note, this means that #girlslikeus who are navigating more than one type of oppression will usually be far more visible as trans people. This reality is reflected in the increased violence, oppression, and discrimination that, say, trans women of colour deal with than white trans women.[23]

2. Fe -- Been contemplating this since the first time you used the term intersection/intersectionality. Do you reference the person who coined the term? I feel like she should be referenced.

It also doesn't help that (as mentioned in the section on medical transition) the WPATH standards of care specify a period of time 'living' as your gender, which often translates — in practice — as doing your absolute best to embody the kind of womanhood reserved for cis women.

None of this addresses the situation of the people who leave the community and assimilate fully to cis society.

What of them? The interesting thing I've noticed about these people who've 'assimilated' is that it appears many of them stay in contact with the trans community just enough to police other people's identities and life choices. Okay.

Obviously, this is a problem. A big problem. The sort of 'having your cake and eating it too' problem. See. If you think the ultimate trans goal is to appear indistinguishable from cis women, never disclose your history, and stop participating in the community? Fine. Do as you will. But you really should stay out of the community. No more policing. No more pushing your assimilationist and normative agenda. Just. GTFO. Okay?

3. b. -- omg, you are 100% right about this. i started this long before i saw some of the recent critiques of non-Black ppl using the term. i'm going to both cite and go back to see how i'm using this term and whether or not it is appropriate. Okay, so I actually ended up removing all mentions and usages of intersectionality within the book. My rubric was this: could the word 'intersection' be substituted for another word with no loss of meaning? If the answer was 'yes' it got removed. And a lose of meaning would mean that whatever I was talking about would stop centering the experiences of Black women -- which any use of intersectionality ought to be explicitly about. See [Strugglingtobeheard about this](http://strugglingtobeheard.tumblr.com/post/66215290586/like-being-very-clear-when-i-asked-patricia-hill)

8. trans IDs only white ppl
are now learning exist

8.1 whiteness as default

Now. This isn't the actual title of Teich's chapter. Nope. He picks 'lesser-known types of transgenderism'[1]. Okay. Genderqueer and non-binary type stuff is included there. So are drag queens.

Okay. To whom is 'genderqueer' and non-binary IDs lesser known? White binary ppl? His wording for this chapter is amusing because he does, at one point, actually mention Two-Spirit and some other global 'trans' identities. Okay. While i'm definitely not asserting that these are genderqueer identities, but i'd say that genderqueerness (for those who ID that way) has actually been well known in many iaopoc communities **before** anyone knew about 'transsexualism' or whatever.

More importantly, the ppl who **are** genderqueer know themselves, I'm sure (at least enough to ID that way).

Of course, this isn't surprising from a person who is making such a strong (and arbitrary) distinction between 'transsexualism' and 'transgenderism'.

1. Teich 2012, 114

8.2 genderqueer and non-binary IDs

8.2.1 Transitionary genders

Teich starts off with the age old box situation. That you have to check 'm' or 'f' and only those. Okay. Whatever. Then, of course, he goes on to assert:

Transsexualism, or transitioning from one sex to another... is only one type of transgenderism[1]

Okay. We've already covered why this distinction is bullshit (and why, for fuck's sake, the use of 'sex' in this context is both gross and unnecessary).

But there are serious, serious problems with the way that he frames genderqueer:

> This does not mean that this person is perpetually confused about gender identity. He or she may feel genderqueer permanently; in other words, it is not always a stepping stone to full transition. People can be perfectly clear that their gender is genderqueer, and that is how they live their lives. At the same time, genderqueer is a common stopover for those who are not sure whether or not they are going to transition and are trying to figure out their true gender identity. [footnote]Teich 2012, 115

This is a serious misrepresentation of what genderqueer means and how many genderqueer people embody their gender and manage their transitions[2]. The confusion here is also exactly why his distinction between 'transsexual' and 'transgender' is not only incorrect, but harmful.

Transitioning isn't (or doesn't have to be) about moving from one 'sex' to another. Genderqueer people transition. Their paths may not be covered by the WPATH standards of (un)care, but they exist. And

---

1. Teich 2012, 114[/foonote].

2. Also? Good job buddy starting with binary pronouns. Would it really have been hard to use the neutral 'they'?

they do what they need to access that transition. And there isn't any defined path because individuals take the path that suits their needs. And some don't 'transition' in the way that Teich uses the word.

More to the point, this implicitly presents the genderqueer identity as sort of the bisexuality of gender, such that it isn't a 'real' identity and whatever. That people use it to take a step out of the gender closet to get a the lay of the land. Now, this is necessary because this is a 'simple guide to a complex topic'.

But. It is actually not at all complicated to assert that people have complex relationships with their gender and their bodies and their communities. That people change over time. That sometimes people are actually coerced into making compromises to access health care (something he should know). That there are a million different reasons for a person IDing as gq at one point in their lives and having some other ID at other points.[3]

8.2.2 Pronouns (really not that difficult)
It sort of boggles my mind that one of the things that ppl apparently have the hardest time with is pronouns. Like it is hard enough getting them to switch from one binary pronoun to another. But it is even harder to get them to even use something like singular 'they'[4]. Teich makes his.... well, almost eye-rolling at the notion of ppl using pronouns other than 'he' or 'she' pretty clear.

> Some will prefer to use only names and no pronouns, which can become awkward: 'Jamie went to the store today. Jamie bought some grapes and oranges, then Jamie brought them out to Jamie's car.' Well, you get the point.

3. Fe -- YES!!!! like actually having been that gender at one point, and then no longer being that gender. Oh, my god I hope I never meet this guy! But, I mean this is that white stagnation. You are x, y, z and were actually only forced to be d, or didn't know you were x so you thought you were d. And this is also that individualist mindset that prevents people from seeing the way you can be xyz, together, not separations and become aft on top of that. But, I mean, what should I expect from a theory that needs separations between gender and sexual orientation.

4. And, no I'm not going to discuss whether or not it is grammatical. Because if compliance to arbitrary grammar rules is more important to you than respecting a person, then you have great issues than can't be solved by grammar.

> Using any alternative pronouns besides he or she requires
> a lot of time and effort in terms of explaining them. [5]

Oh. Okay. But not really. Do they really take that much time and effort to explain (and, by extension, to learn and use)? Is it really all that awkward to use a person's name instead of a pronoun? Not really. He really glosses over the more probable reason why a non-binary person might let random strangers misgender them in public...

It isn't because these things are difficult to explain. This is simple substitution. Instead of 'he' use 'ey'[6]. Really not that hard.

However, the probable motivation for this is that it can be incredibly dangerous to disclose your trans status to random people on the street. Who, not because of the difficulty of understanding pronouns, might respond in transmisogynist ways because they actually just fucking hate you. [7]

Just a thought.

8.2.3 Gender variant or gender non-conforming?

> Any transgender person can be considered gender variant
> or gender nonconforming because he or she, by definition,
> does not conform to Western society's notion of what a
> male or female is.[8]

Lol. No. Sorry. 'By definition', yes, his definition. Which we've already pointed out is wrong. Recall the working definition for this book:

Transgender: A hegemonic socio-political identity crafted by (mostly) , binary trans people.

---

5. Teich 2012, 116

6. And, yes, there are people with cognitive reasons for having a bit of trouble. I've not met a single non-binary person who doesn't understand this. Fuck. I understand it because I cannot remember words that I can't pronounce. So there is a whole set of pronouns that I've only read but never heard, so I have a lot of trouble, online, remembering them. All it means is that I put extra effort into it. Something I'm **happy** to do, as it demonstrates my respect for the person I'm talking to.

7. Fe -- word.

8. Teich 2012, 117

So, I suppose this doesn't necessarily contradict his claim, since part of his hegemonic understanding of transgender is that all of them are gender variant. Okay. I still don't know why he has issues with the sex/gender distinction. But. Whatever.

I don't really know what to make of the rest of his discussion. Are dmab ppl more often called gender nonconforming? I can't say. I mean, no one used this when I was growing up. It was all 'faggot' and related terms.

8.3 Crossdressers

I've been thinking about 'drag queens' and 'crossdressers' for a little while and how the conception of these two practices can be understood in the larger colonial context that erases, devalues, destroys trans feminine poc genderessence.

I recently saw another person from the place spanish people called the Philippines define Asog as the 'Sacred Drag Queen.'[1] Now, coming from them and in this context (i.e., the spiritual role that bakla used to serve in different 'Filipin@' ethnic groups), I don't mind this translation, even as it fascinates me (but fuck any and all white people who saw bakla and dismissed us as being 'drag queens').

That it could be construed that 'bakla = Tagalog drag queen' is interesting for me for the way it invokes the performativity of the gender role in ways that I'm sure is likely making many a white trans person squirm as they read this (if there are any). Because... the butlerian gender theory of performance is usually hated because of the way that it implies that gender isn't real. (and I get why).

But there are cultures (mine for example) where the gender is, at least in part, a performative role in the sense that the gender is not only defined by what it is but what it does. It is/was about the role you played in your community. I guess, to put it in a different way, your gender was/is relational and not necessarily just a personal, 'private' thing (and, yeah, can we also recognize this notion of personal vs. public as a different invention of white colonialism?). [2]

What I find so interesting about the ways that the white colonizers came to discuss the 'cross dressing' of the Indigenous people they encountered, is how it reveals just how deeply they misunderstood

1. http://urbananito.wikispaces.com/Worldview+%26+Value+System#Worldview & Value System--Tribal Roles & Folklore Personas

2. nica -- just a note: Butler also argues against a 'subject' that is prior to gender, who does or performs gender as a kind of choice -- however, her argument reduces gender to an effect of coercive regimes, which, yeah, is deeply ahistorical and euro-centric because it does nothing to bring up the things you are mentioning here, gender as relational in ways and contexts prior to or in opposition to white modernity

what it was they were seeing and just how white supremacist their world views are. Because describing the people they encountered as 'cross dressers' implied the existence of a binary that didn't exist. It was a term that invalidated and trivialized the trans feminine people they were applying it to.

HOWEVER

What I'm not getting at, at all, is the way that white cross dressing men like to go 'We are still men and not gross and icky like those trans women' because those people are trans misogynistic as fuck and can choke on their trans panic.

Because my real point is not about whether or not trans feminine Indigenous genders are 'crossdressers' but how this framework, as applied to us, misses the point and is white supremacist. As well as trans misogynist. It also helps create the inapplicable hierarchy of 'real' women and men who wear woman's clothing by making it only about personal ID and removing the relational role that our identities served in the communities.

Because, self ID matters but so does/did the role we occupied in our communities.

And it is important to remember that while we remained ourselves, what was taken is the role we occupied. This is or must be an integral part of how we conceive of decolonization: remembering that our selves and our IDs aren't just personal, private affairs with no relationship to our community.

That also creating an artificial division between cross dressers and women is something that was imposed from the outside... since an Asog who puts on certain kinds of clothing usually worn by women to serve a ceremonial or ritualistic role as part of a spiritual practice is no less valid or real from the Asog who embodies that role all the time.

The creation of an ID of 'crossdresser' interests me because... for those before the ability to use medical technologies to better embody yourself, it is likely that a combination of clothing/adornment + social recognition was how you came to embody your role.

(And I refuse to speculate whether, if given the option, a bakla of 500 years ago would choose to avail themselves of modern day medical technology because it entirely misses the point.)

8.4 Intersex

I'm not going to get into this, since I'm not intersex and I have no place really to speak on their behalf.

Instead, I want to highlight some of the tensions between the Intersex community and the trans community (insofar as 'community' in this case is being understood of the Intersex people who do not also ID as trans and vice versa). I mainly want to point out two large failures in the discourse and organizing.

8.4.1 Trans ppl using Intersex bodies as rhetorical points

This is commonly used as a trump card of some kind when people are debating the realities of lived gender and sex.

Person A will make some kind of biological essentialist argument rooted in genetics, and the trans person will go:

"Aha! You are wrong because Intersex people!"

Which is an entirely shitty thing to do because Intersex bodies are not what we should be stepping on for trans liberation.

Doing this actively hurts and damages Intersex people.

8.4.2 Intersex ppl capitalising on the medicalisation of gender

This usually involves Intersex people making rhetorical moves of this kind:

"I deserve to have my gender recognised, surgery paid for, etc. because I have a legitimate medical condition!"

They are able to mobilise general public sympathy and influence policy by feeding into the general medicalisation of gender. It also serves to explicitly and rhetorically move their struggle for rights and recognition away from trans ppl's.

It is harmful because the medicalisation of gender tends to disproportionately impact #girlslikeus.

8.5 Teh Binary

8.5.1 Binarism and Colonialism

I want to have a talk about binarism. But with some serious shifts in the discussion because what I've no interest in saying is:

> 1. That binary trans people have anything to do with a special oppression for non-binary people.
> 2. That white non-binary people have any special kind of oppression, i.e., that binarism is something that impacts PoC exclusively.
> 3. That, if binarism is a thing, that this means that binary trans people have any less right to defend their communities and protect themselves from either non-binary or cis people. This goes double for binary TPoC.
> 4. That binarism, if real, is a thing related to colonialism and racism (although, I'm still trying to think if it is distinct from just racism and colonialism — I think so but not quite sure how to say why).
> 5. I want to do all of the above without erasing the very real nature of passing privilege and what I might call ethnic heritage privilege (something I use very reluctantly 'cause I'm referring to PoC cultures, but I think there is some relative privilege here).

In some ways, I'm sort of saying that I think binarism is a real problem, but not from a trans on trans thing, but actually more of a white vs. PoC axis.

First, that image with the comment that it is most of white, white-passing, or lightskin people who ID as genderqueer bothered me because of the way that it completely ignored/erased those PoC cultures where non-binary or third genders (if I may be excused for using this problematic term) exist. I realize it may have been referring to what goes down in canada, the us, or europe, but the effect is still the same. 'Cause all ranges of skin tones will represent in non-binary PoC IDs, particularly if they live in the country of cultural origin (i.e., Nepalese in Nepal or Filipin@s in the Philippines).

But what I do want to say is that binarism is a tool of colonialism (like racism). I think it was created by white cis people to oppress non-binary PoC. In the cases I'm talking about passing privilege isn't an issue because some (but not all) bakla aren't about passing and it is, specifically, our perceived inability to pass that made 'ladyboy' the (somewhat dated) translation for bakla (which more recently has come to mean 'gay').

(but this process of meaning shifting from ladyboy to gay is, itself, a result of a binarist colonial process that erases and delegitimizes not only the bakla who pass and, thus, often just ID as women, but also those bakla who pass, but don't ID as women, those who are effete gay men, those who are butch, etc. It is a means to reduce the rich diversity and complexity that exists in Filipin@ culture into anglo, binary terms.)

Asians queers (heck, all Asians) are expected to be femme, docile, etc. These are issues of racism, but I think that these racist stereotypes also include colonial, binary notions of gender which are used against PoC.

(which, I suddenly realize I'm contradicting myself 'cause I said it was for non-binary PoC but now I'm saying it might be all PoC)

That binarism is connected to colonialism is important for how white people represented PoC cultures in their history books, because they sought to represent us using their binary constructions of gender.

This process I'm talking about, is also at the heart of the larger criticism that white/light-skin/white passing people are usually only seen as IDing as genderqueer. And the special snowflake status they seek because they wish to implicate other trans people, as well as cis people. Moreover, it is problematic the way that white genderqueer people can be seen to fetishize, romanticize, and appropriate non-binary PoC IDs.

I think the consequences are very different for non-binary Poc and non-binary white people. Whiteness as, from the moment it encountered us, sought to erase, eradicate, or explain away non-binary PoC. It was part of the colonial/missionary project.

(and while it may be argued that it was homophobia informing this process, not a particular kind of non-binary specific transphobia, I'm not convinced that this can be supported. That americans, since I think it was them, coined the term ladyboy to mock and degrade bakla or — more recently — kathoey, when they could have just used queer or faggot somewhat indicates that they recognized a qualitative difference between what we bakla are and what they understood queers/faggots to be.)

Part of what I tend to agree with, is that a case needs to be made that something counts as its own oppression, as opposed to being part of a different oppressive axis. Also, I feel the body count criteria is good. On this note, while I don't have receipts because I've not done the research at this point, I have zero doubts that when colonizers have been in any cultural group that recognizes third or non-binary genders, those people have been killed, murdered, demonized, etc. Part of what I'm working from here is how ladyboy is a slur. And no one who is a ladyboy is passing and while white sex tourists in the Philippines may do violence against bakla, I don't think it can adequately be explained by transmisogyny or transphobia. [1]

1. nica -- this is just some thoughts i'm having. nothing special really. and not necessarily a comment on this part. but. maybe. and i think since whiteness is a project of humanity. or humanity a project of whiteness. that this simultanous disavowal and desire for bakla (as you mention below, the fetishistic appeal is in being neither ((white)) men nor women) might have to do with the literal use of this incoherence of bakla, to whiteness, as a way of reconstituting the borders of the self, or a way of knowing one self as white/human against and through the incoherency or obliteration of the other. not to reduce this to a self/other dillema or dynamic solely informed by that crisis, but i think you're right that maybe transmisogyny and transphobia alone don't/can't hold or adequately explain this. and, i'm thinking of tiffany king's work, stating black women's bodies were seen as useful in any way 'imaginable' or 'unimaginable' by the white-settler-master. the pleasure in knowing the other as malleable object for one's desires -- not to say that black woman's ontology is comparable to anyone else's --eric stanley, a white queer, in a way attempts to address anti-queer violence by analyzing queer as a signifier empty of meaning, but he so fails by not specifying the genealogy of violence against trans feminine iaopoc that you're investigating in your book. but i think it may have something to do w this. white ppl undestanding themself by being able to map whatever meaning onto other bodies. which, yeah, white supremacy. idk maybe this comment is helpful in some way? -- backtracking, i just read part of what you've written below. so yes, binarism as a necessary response to the 'incoherence' of indigenous genders, as a marker of white humanity, and as a method of elimination. and as an ongoing project. and the desire violence fetishism that is part of this project ... in the historical sense of initial contact/early settlement and its continuation to the now

Part of the fetishistic appeal of ladyboys is that we are not women and we are not men.

In conclusion, I think binarism is a real thing. At least if we are talking in the context of colonialism and racism. I have my doubts about its relevance and realness if we are talking about white genderqueers.

8.5.2 Binaryism: Myths and Realities

The pieces of how i conceive of binarism are sort of spread out amongst various posts. But, based on a twitter convo, it is time to make a single post that ties in all of these elements together.

Before I start, I'm going to get these statements out of the way:

> 1. Any white person invoking binarism as something they experience is transmisogynist.
> 2. It is categorically impossible for any trans feminine Indigenous and/or Person of Colour to be 'binarist'.
> 3. Binarism should be properly understood as a sub-privilege of whiteness, with a focus on gender.

Okay. I wrote about the connection between the gender binary and colonialism in the previous section. The major takeaway for this post is that the 'binary' is best understood as one of the many colonial tools white people used to subjugate, colonize, kill, etc. Indigenous and/or People of Colour the world over.

White non-binary people attempt to make a claim that binarism is primarily about gender, that any and all binary people have privilege over them and, conversely, are participants in a system that oppresses non-binary people. This, of course, is complete and total bullshit. It is especially bullshit because you often see these (often dfab) non-binary white people weaponize this concept against trans women. Which is, of course, transmisogynist. Even the assertion that non-binary dfab trans people experience a similar type of 'binarism' to dmab non-binary people is transmisogynist.

But if I'm correct about the binary being an important part of colonialism and gender oppression in general, then the other take away is that all white people benefit from the binary, inasmuch as they benefit from colonialism.

The binary as a construct of whiteness, as needed upon the moment that white settlers and colonizers encountered Indigenous people embodying genders that were largely incoherent to them. The binary became necessary at this point so that they could: first, conceptualize these unknown and incoherent genders, second, that once 'understood' they could work to eradicate these genders.

Note: this is the birth of transmisogyny as well. Since, as we know from history, white people at these early stages and for centuries to come and up to now, where entirely and completely focused on the trans feminine. It is our bodies they recorded into their travelogues, our bodies the examined so that they could determine who we were (hint: men wearing women's clothing!!!), it is our bodies that they began to leverage essentialized notions of what it is to be a man or woman, our bodies that they sought to destroy and erase from history (even as they maintained their lurid curiousity).

White people needed a strictly enforced binary in order to dislocate people with indigenous genders from the roles we held in our communities. And it was absolutely necessary that this occur because, for many of the communities, people embodying these genders often had some spiritual function. The importance of religion both at this point in history and right now should not be misunderstood. Spiritual leaders/participants/practitioners have always held power. Christianity (often catholicism) is and was major component of the colonial enterprise. And it was necessary as a means of control over indigenous populations.

So. We are talking about the birth of the binary and transmisogyny. Important to remember that we are talking about the birth of the institutions established to oppress people. And to privilege some over others. Not talking about the birth of the concepts themselves.

What does all of this mean in terms of today?

Well, white people being what they are, have created a notion of binarism that claims that people embodying 'binary' genders have institutional power/privilege over people who do not embody a 'binary' gender.

And, of course, this ahistorical notion of binarism ends up positioning the people whom are most impacted by transmisogyny as somehow oppressive to people who are, in many cases, not impacted by transmisogyny at all. This is absurd. And it is also not just transmisogynist in its own right, but racist.

There is literally no conceivable way to frame a Black and/or Latin@ trans woman as somehow wielding privilege over non-binary white people. In fact, framing a IaoPoC trans woman as 'binary' or 'non-binary' is white supremacist.

Because, the binary as tool of oppression is not about legitimizing binary genders over non-binary genders, in a general sense, but about legitimizing a white notion of manhood and a white notion of womanhood. And, in turn, this is inextricably tied to who is considered 'human' and who isn't.

As in:

There are only two kinds of human beings: white men and white women.

The binary serves to centre the white, colonial gender system. It serves to forcibly make it the comprehensive framework in which we view all gender. This is exactly why calling any trans feminine IaoPoC 'binary' or 'non-binary' is white supremacist. It forcibly places their genders inside a white gender system. It pushes forward the myth that IaoPoC genders are only comprehensible within whiteness. That, otherwise, these genders do not exist.

So. What of 'binary' privilege? How can we conceptualize it with this history in mind and with an understanding of what the binary is for?

I mentioned above that I consider 'binary privilege' to be a subset of white privilege, as such all white people benefit from it.

Yes. I am including non-binary white people. To be very explicit:

white non-binary people benefit from the binary.

Of course, this also means that binary white people likewise benefit.

If the binary is, in part, what legitimizes the white gender system as being the only valid why to conceptualize and articulate gender, then all white genders achieve legitimacy within this system that is impossible for any trans feminine IaoPoC.

This is why, the womanhood of binary white trans women is more legitimate than the womanhood of a trans woman of colour.

But note: this is also how white non-binary genders obtain greater legitimacy than a putatively 'binary' trans woman of colour.

White non-binary genders, being helpfully entrenched within the white gender system, are coherent in ways that IaoPoC gender never is.

The above is exactly how and why non-binary white people have been able to leverage and weaponize 'binarism' against trans feminine people of colour. Because while, sure, they can likely make some claim that their identities are not considered legitimate in relation to a binary cis person, but that doesn't change the fact that their identity is more legitimate than a 'binary' trans woman of colour.

So, to answer a question about the notion that only cis genders are legitimate and trans genders are not, yes. Of course this is true. But, when we consider race as a fundamental aspect of embodied gendered experiences, we must also understand that there are gradations of illegitimacy.

A cis white person's gender is legitimate.

A white trans woman's gender is illegitimate.

A white non-binary person's gender is also illegitimate.

A trans woman of colour's gender is less legitimate than both the white cis person, the white trans woman, and the white non-binary person.

Which answers another question. A white trans woman has no systemic privilege over a white non-binary person. But both of them do have systemic privilege over a trans woman of colour. And, yes, while we can simply reduce this white privilege — which I'm totally fine with, it should not be forgotten that one of the privileges of whiteness is having a gender that is defacto more legitimate and more coherent because of the binary framework in which it necessarily exists.

To put in another way, binary privilege is that part of white privilege which allows white people to continuously centre their genders and their voices.

Binarism, thus, is also a white trans woman acting as if her experiences with transmisogyny are equivalent to that of a Black and/or Latin@ trans woman's, despite the piles of evidence that white trans women are not experiencing the most violent and damaging expressions of transmisogyny.

Binarism, thus, is also a white non-binary person using claims of 'binarism' to excuse their transmisogyny.

8.5.3 On nonbinary 'invisibility'

nica recently shared with me this thing of some non-binary person asserting that 'trans(asterisk)' was something that only non-binary people should use. and that binary trans ppl using that are erasing nonbinary ppl? Or that not using it is erasing nonbinary people? i can't really reconstruct this argument because it was absurd and i was busy laughing.

anyway.

in terms of calls for inclusion and calls for action from the nonbinary community, the topic of visibility often comes up. visibility is one of those really pernicious notions because not only do most people misunderstand what visibility is about (or ought to be about) but because they most often see _hyper visibility_ and, in their bitter envy, decide that _this_ is what their goal should be and something worth working towards.

of course, this is _wrong_. Hyper-visibility is not a desirable thing. Ask any Black person. And this topic of visibility often comes up in racial discussions. light-skin mixed-with-white poc (like me) will come out and be all "i'm poc tooooooo! and no one pays attention to my experiences of racism!!!!!!". and it is simply fucking ridiculous and _always_ ends up mobilizing anti-Blackness in some important way.

the thing about ppl who constantly call for visibility is that they never actually clearly outline…. *who* they want to see them. Whose gaze are they hoping to attract? Who is not seeing them?

so often, the goal appears to be the oppressive gaze. they want to be seen and recognized by power. they want their identities and selves to be given shape and form in the eyes of their oppressors. they appear to legitimately think that, unless power sees them, they don't exist. [2]

and that this is what is desired is clear when these ppl constantly point to hyper visiable groups as examples of people who are 'visible,' who have the 'privilege' of being seen by power. they point to these groups and talk about how we (in the case of trans women) take up too much space and don't allow others to be seen???.

except that hyper visibility is surveillance. it is dissection. it is violation. it is what allows so many of us to die and mostly by virtue of our deaths, become 'visible.' the fact that i'm seen, is often why i can't fucking bring myself to leave the house.

moreover

these nonbinary people are often fucking _wrong_ about their level of visibility. and it doesn't surprise me that i most often see this coming from white people, which is kinda amusing given that white nonbinary ppl actually _benefit_ from the binary (as noted in the previous section). but all these white nonbinary ppl dying to be seen by the oppressive gaze…

not realizing that, actually, 'nonbinary' ppl have been **visible** for centuries. that out in the colonies where transmisogyny and binarism was born, and white ppl were busy coercively naming some of us as 'third genders[3]'

---

2. Fe -- oh, god, this is strumming my pain right now. I'm rarely embarrassed, but this was me. I was really, really snorting that white powder.

3. http://biyuti.com/blog/totally-didnt-know-third-gender-was-a-culture-specific-appropriateable-thing-whats-the-history-of-the-term/

THAT 'NONBINARY' PPL HAVE BEEN VISIBLE TO POWER FOR CENTURIES AND DYING BECAUSE OF THIS

and we are _still_ dying. and often dying not only via transmisogyny, cissexism, and binarism, but dying as part of larger projects of colonialism and genocide. from which: white nonbinary ppl are reaping many hearty benefits.

but of course, instead of, idk, fucking _realizing_ any of this, fucking white (and often dfab) nonbinary ppl are too busy eating the shit of patriarchy and colonialism to give even a solitary fuck about the ppl in 'their community' dying and suffering because of the visibility they crave and envy.

Conclusions

9.1 Final thoughts

So. I'm sitting here after having sloppily edited and quickly read through most of the book and I don't really know what to say for conclusions. i mean... lol, i hope everyone can forgive the fact that i repeated a few points in a few different sections. although, i do tend to think that it creates a level of flow and coherence that, for the most part, isn't really present in the book.

i guess i want to leave this with the thought/reminder that deconstructing/decolonizing white trans/gender theory and practise is necessary.

Necessary because i know that in the PH, targetting trans feminine people (bayot, asog, etc.) was a necessary part of colonization. it was necessary to convert people to catholocism. it was necessary to enforce the binary and the patriarchy, it was one of the ways that the spaniards targetted women and made us... less than we were.

necessary because hundreds of years later...

we are still here. our status may be low and degraded from what we used to be.

but we have survived.

any meaningful steps towards decolonization will need to grapple with who we once were and who we are now. it will need to recognize the importance of our struggle and the importance of **us** within the community.

above all: i want us to be free.

Bibliography

"About the San Francisco Trans March | San Francisco Trans March." Accessed February 9, 2014. http://www.transmarch.org/about.

binaohan, b. "On the Socialization of Bodies." Oh, the Hu-manatee!, November 3, 2013. http://share.biyuti.com/post/65889617756.

—. "Q&A with Biyuti." Oh, the Hu-manatee!, November 3, 2013. http://share.biyuti.com/post/65905892490.

"Binarism and Colonialism – Biyuti." Accessed February 9, 2014. http://biyuti.com/blog/binarism-and-colonialism/.

"Binarism: Myths and Reality – Biyuti." Accessed February 9, 2014. http://biyuti.com/blog/binarism-myths-and-reality/.

Brewer, Carolyn. "Intersections: Baylans, Asogs, Transvestism, and Sodomy: Gender, Sexuality and the Sacred in Early Colonial Philippines." Intersections: Gender, History and Culture in the Asian Context no. 2 (1999). http://intersections.anu.edu.au/issue2/carolyn2.html.

Dauvergne, Mia, and Shannon Brennan. "Police-reported Hate Crime in Canada, 2009." Statistics Canada. Accessed September 13, 2013. http://www.statcan.gc.ca/pub/85-002-x/2011001/article/11469-eng.htm#a3.

D'orsay, Toni. Introduction to Transness – Complete. Accessed August 20, 2013. http://www.dyssonance.com/wp-content/uploads/2013/08/Introduction-to-Transness.pdf.

—. "Untitled." Dyssonance, July 20. http://tonidorsay.tumblr.com/post/55995980361/ciscritical-not-cisphobic-sapphisms-replied-to.

Haraway, Donna. "A Cyborg Manifesto." Accessed June 14, 2013. http://www.egs.edu/faculty/donna-haraway/articles/donna-haraway-a-cyborg-manifesto/.

"Injustice at Every Turn: A Report of the National Transgender Discrimination Survey." Accessed April 4, 2013. http://www.thetaskforce.org/reports_and_research/ntds.

Norris, Denise. "TransGriot: On Being Transgender." Accessed April 4, 2013. http://transgriot.blogspot.ca/2011/12/on-being-transgender.html.

"On Nonbinary 'Invisibility' – Biyuti." Accessed February 9, 2014. http://biyuti.com/blog/on-nonbinary-invisibility/.

"Private Member's Bill – Bill C-279 – Third Reading (41-2)." Accessed February 9, 2014. http://www.parl.gc.ca/HousePublications/Publication.aspx?Language=E&Mode=1&DocId=6256603&File=24#1.

Roberts, Monica. "Stealth Doesn't Help The Trans Community." TransGriot. Accessed July 21, 2013. http://transgriot.blogspot.ca/2013/07/stealth-doesnt-help-trans-community.html.

—. "TransGriot: On Being Transgender – Part II." Accessed February 9, 2014. http://transgriot.blogspot.ca/2011/12/on-being-transgender-part-ii.html.

"Sexual Orientation and Gender Identity: Terminology and Definitions | Resources." Human Rights Campaign. Accessed February 9, 2014. http://www.hrc.org/resources/entry/sexual-orientation-and-gender-identity-terminology-and-definitions.

Strugglingtobeheard. "like being very clear, when i asked Patricia Hill Collins about the co-opting of her terms and the use of white feminisms use of intersectionality as a feminist theory she had CHOICE words". Accessed May 7, 2014. http://strugglingtobeheard.tumblr.com/post/66215290586/like-being-very-clear-when-i-asked-patricia-hill

Teich, Nicholas M. Transgender 101: a Simple Guide to a Complex Issue. Columbia University Press, 2012.

The Danger of a Single Story. Accessed February 9, 2014. http://www.ted.com/talks/chimamanda_adichie_the_danger_of_a_single_story.html.

"Totally Didn't Know Third Gender Was a Culture-specific, Appropriateable Thing. What's the History of the Term? – Biyuti." Accessed February 9, 2014. http://biyuti.com/blog/totally-didnt-know-third-gender-was-a-culture-specific-appropriateable-thing-whats-the-history-of-the-term/.

"Transgender Day of Remembrance." Wikipedia, the Free Encyclopedia, January 23, 2014. http://en.wikipedia.org/w/index.php?title=Transgender_Day_of_Remembrance&oldid=582700561.

"TransGriot: Why The Transgender Community Hates HRC." Accessed February 9, 2014. http://transgriot.blogspot.ca/2007/10/why-transgender-community-hates-hrc.html.
Tuck, Eve, and K. Wayne Yang. "Decolonization Is Not a Metaphor." Decolonization: Indigeneity, Education & Society 1, no. 1 (2012): 1-40.

"Update on 'Trans Feminine' – Biyuti." Accessed February 9, 2014. http://biyuti.com/blog/update-on-trans-feminine/.

Valentine, David, and ebrary, Inc. Imagining Transgender an Ethnography of a Category. Durham: Duke University Press, 2007. http://site.ebrary.com/lib/ubc/Doc?id=10243714.

"Why 'Trans Feminine'…. – Biyuti." Accessed February 9, 2014. http://biyuti.com/blog/why-trans-feminine/.

about the publisher

biyuti publishing is a twoc-centric publishing alternative (doors are also open to all qtpoc). We are community run and operating with a different kind of publishing business model.

And, I mean, we have the actual *best* logo. Look at this manatee, LOOK AT IT.

CPSIA information can be obtained at www.ICGtesting.com
Printed in the USA
LVOW10s0021110815

449560LV00005B/948/P